LENA
BEFORE AND AFTER LUTEFISK

Compiled and Edited by
Charlene Power

Illustrated by Charlene Power
Printed by Barbo-Carlson Enterprises
Box 189, Lindsborg, KS 67456-0189
Published by Charlene Power
Box 204, Crosby, North Dakota 58730 0209
Phone: (701) 965-6648

Soft Cover Edition ISBN: 0-944996-29-9

First Printing: October 2002

Copyright © 2002 by Charlene Power

Lena took Ole to the doctor and was waiting patiently for the doctor's diagnosis. Finally, the doctor called Lena into his office.

"Lena, I just don't like the look of him," said the doctor with a sad look on his face.

"Vell, doc, I don't eider," replied Lena. "But he is good tew da shildren!!!"

*** *** ***

Ole and Lars were out fishing when their boat capsized!! Lars couldn't swim but Ole quickly swam to shore. Just as soon as he got there he jumped right back into the lake.

"Vat are yew doing Ole?" yelled the bystanders.

"Vell vat dew yew tink dat I am doing?" hollered Ole."I yust saved myself and now I'm going back in tew save Lars!!!"

*** *** ***

Sven decided to take a walk one fine morning and he walked past Ole's house. Hanging on a big tree was a sign that said 'Boat Fer Sale!' This really confused Sven because he knew that Ole didn't own a boat!! So he went up and knocked on Ole's door.

"Hey, Ole," said Sven. "I noticed yer sign dat says 'Boat Fer Sale.' But Ole, yew don't even have a boat!!! All dat yew have is yer old Yohn Deer tractor and da combine!!!"

"Vell, ya sure!!

I know dat fer sure and dere boat fer sale!!!!" Ole quickly replied.

*** *** ***

Poor Hilda passed away and the excited Lars called 911! The operator told Lars that she would send someone out right away!!

"Lars?" she asked. "Where do you live?"

"Vell, ve live at da end of Eucalyptus Drive," replied Lars.

"Can you spell that for me?" asked the operator.

There was a very long pause!

Finally Lars said, "Vell, how about if I drag her over tew Oak Street and yew can pick her up dere?"

*** *** ***

Ingvald was invited over to his friend Knute's house one night for dinner. Knute was a wonderful host and Ingvald couldn't help but notice that each time he addressed his wife he used endearing terms... calling her Honey, Sweetheart, Darling and Pumpkin, etc!!

Inga left the room to bring in the dessert and Ingvald said, "It is so nice dat after all dese years dat yew and Inga have been married dat yew are still calling her dose pet names!!!"

Knute quickly pulled him aside and hung his head!! "Vell, tew tell yew da trut, I fergot her name tree years ago!!!!!!"

*** *** ***

"Come along now," said St. Peter. "Your home is backed right up to this beautiful championship golf course!! You will have golfing privileges every day!!! Also, each week the golf course will be changed to a new one, representing all of the greatest golf courses in the world!!!"

"Vell, how much are da green fees?" asked Ole.

"You play for FREE!!!" said St. Peter. "THIS IS HEAVEN!"

Next they went to the clubhouse and there was a lavish buffet lunch with beautiful food from around the world!!!

"How much does it cost tew eat?" asked Ole.

"Don't yew understand, Ole!!" asked St. Peter. "IT'S FREE!! THIS IS HEAVEN!!!"

"Vell, den vhere are da low fat and low colesterol tables?" asked Lena timidly.

"That's the best part!!!" said St. Peter. "You can eat as much as you like and you'll never get fat and you'll never get sick!!! THIS IS HEAVEN!!!"

With that announcement Ole went into a fit of rage!!! He threw down his hat and stomped on it, shrieking wildly!!! Lena and St. Peter both tried to calm him down!!

"Vell, Ole!! Vat is wrong vit yew?" asked poor embarrassed Lena!

"VELL, LENA!!" yelled Ole. "DIS IS ALL YER FAULT, LENA!!! IF IT HADN'T BEEN FER DOS BLASTED BRAN MUFFINS OF YERS, I COULD HAVE BEEN HERE 10 YEARS AGO!!!!"

Osama bin Laden was sitting in his cave, plotting terrorist strategy when his telephone rang!!

"Hello, Mr. bin Laden," said a heavily accented voice. "Dis is Ole down at da Viking Pub in Ringebu, Norvay. I am ringing tew inform yer dat ve are officially declaring var on yew!!!"

"Well, Ole," Osama replied. "This indeed important news! How big is your army?"

"Vell, right now," said Ole, after a few minutes calculation, "dere is myself, my cousin Engebert, my next door neighbor, Lars, and da entire drinking club from da pub!!! Dat makes eight!!!"

Osama takes a long pause! "I must tell you, Ole, that I have a million men in my army waiting to move on my command."

"Vell, Uff-da!" said Ole. "I'll have tew call yew back!!"

Sure enough, the next day, Ole called again.

"Mr. bin Laden! Da var is still on! Ve have managed to get some infantry equipment!!"

"And what equipment would that be, Ole?" asked Osama.

"Vell, ve have two combines, a bulldozer, Lars's farm tractor and five lefse rollers!!" replied Ole.

Osama sighed!!! "I must tell you this, Ole. I have 16,000 tanks and 14,000 armored personal carriers. Also, I have increased my army by 1½ million since we last spoke!!!"

"Double Uff-da!!!" said Ole. "I vill have tew get back tew yew!!!"

Sure enough, Ole rang again the next day! "Mr. Bin Laden, da var is still on!! Ve have managed tew get ourselves airborne!!! Ve have modified Engebretsen's ultra-light with a couple of shotguns in the cockpit, and four boys from da Larsdatter's farm have yoined us as vell!!!"

Osama was silent for a minute and then he cleared his throat! "I must tell you, Ole, that I have 10,000 bombers and 20,000 fighter planes! My military complex is surrounded by laser-guided, surface-to-air missile sites. And since we last spoke, I've increased my army to TWO MILLION!!!"

"HOLY SONS OF NORVAY.", said Ole. "I'll have tew call yew back!!!"

Sure enough, Ole called again the next day. "Mornin' Mr. Bin Laden!! I am sorry tew tell yew dat ve have had tew call off da var!!!"

"I'm sorry to hear that, Ole." Said Mr. Bin Laden. "Why the change of heart?"

"Vell," said Ole. "Ve all had a long chat over a bottle of aquavit and ve decided dat dere is no vay dat ve can feed dos two million prisioners!!!!"

*** *** ***

3

The third grade teacher asked if anyone could name all of the states in the United States.

"Oh, ya, sure, Teacher!!" said Little Pete! He rattled them off alphabetically without a mistake!!

"Well, that is just wonderful!!!!" said Miss Jones. "When I was your age I couldn't have named all the states!!!"

"Vell, is dat right?" asked Little Pete. "Uff-da!!! And den dere vere only turteen!!!!"

*** *** ***

The patrolman pulled Olaf over!!! "I noticed that you didn't have a seat belt on a minute ago!" he said.

"Yes, I did," said Olaf. "If yew don't believe me and yew can't take my vord fer it, yust ask my vife!!!"

"So how about it, ma'am?" asked the patrolman.

"Vell, officer! I have been married tew Olaf fer turty years," replied Olga. "And dere is vun ting dat I have learned in all dat time!! It is never argue vit him vhen he is drunk!!!"

*** *** ***

Ole and Lena were sitting out on their front porch in their rockers!! Ole reached over and patted Lena on the knee!!!

"Lena," he said. "Vat ever happened tew our sex relations?"

"Vell, Ole! I yust don't know. I don't tink ve even got a card from any of dem last Christmas!!!"

*** *** ***

The preacher had just finished his sermon when the devil appeared at the pulpit!!! The good minister got a little bit nervous but the devil said, "Continue on with your service. I am just here to check on a few of your parishioners!!"

Everyone in the church jumped up and ran out screaming loudly except for a little old man in the front row!!! (Of course his name was Ole Olson!!)

"Well, Ole!" said the devil. "Why didn't you run out of the church screaming like all the rest of the congregation?"

"Vell!!!" said Ole. "I'm not afraid of yew!!! I've been married tew yer sister fer fifty years!!!!"

*** *** ***

Knute was driving along in his truck and he stops for a red light. Some crazy woman jumps from the car behind him, runs up to the truck, knocks on the door. Knute rolls down the window, and she says, "Hi! My name is Olga from da Carribean and yew are losing some of yer load!!"

"Vell, Uff-da!!" thought Knute. "I'll yust ignore dat crazy voman!!" and he kept right on driving. When he stops for another stop light, the lady jumps out of her car and comes running to his truck again!!! She knocks on the window again!!!

Knute rolls down the window again! "Hi!!" she said. "My name is Olga and you are still losing some of your load!"

Shaking his head, Knute heads on down the street and then again he has to stop at a stop light!! Here comes that crazy woman again!! Of course, he rolls down the window and she says, "Hi! My name is Olga from the Carribean and you are losing your load!!!!"

"Vat's she so excited about!!" thought Knute. So he reved up his truck and raced to the next light. When he stopped this time he quickly jumped out of his truck and raced back to the ladies car! He knocks on the window and as she lowers it he says, "Hi! My name is Knute! It's winter in North Dakota and I'm driving my SALT TRUCK!!!!!"

*** *** ***

Poor grief stricken Peter threw himself on the grave and he cried bitterly!!! "My life is so senseless and how worthless everyting is fer me now dat yew are gone! If only yew hadn't died! If yust fate hadn't been so cruel as tew take yew from dis vorld!! How different everyting vould have been if yew had lived!!!"

Just then a clergyman happened by. To soothe poor Peter, he offered a prayer and then he said, "I assume that the person lying beneath this beautiful headstone is someone of great importance tew yew."

"Importance!!!" declared Peter. "Indeed he vas important! He vas my vife's first husband!!!"

*** *** ***

Sven got a cab in New York City and the cab driver sensed that he was a little nervous so he decided to strike up a conversation!

"My parents had tree kids," said the cab driver. "One was my sister and the other was my brother. Do you know who the third one was?"

"Vell, I sure don't!!" replied Sven.

"It was me!!!" said the laughing driver.

When Sven arrived at home, he decided to try the story out on his wife Hilda.

"My folks had tree kids," he said. "Vun vas my sister and da udder vas my brudder. Now, can yew guess who da turd vun vas, Hilda?"

Poor Hilda thought and thought and finally she had to admit that she didn't know!!

"Vell, Hilda!!! Yew should sure know dat!!! It was some cab driver in New York City!!!"

*** *** ***

Little Hilda was going to the dentist for the first time for a checkup. As they walked into the dentist's office she asked, "MaMa, is dis vhere da toot fairy lives?"

*** *** ***

Ole and Sven decided to go fishing. However, by the time they had cut a hole in the ice big enough for their boat, it was too late and they had to go home!!!

*** *** ***

Queen Lena'as Motto is 'YUST KEEP SMILING'!!! It yust makes everyvun vonder vat yew are up too!!!!!!

*** *** ***

Lena went to a beautiful beach one day and she found a very beautiful bottle!! She was very curious, so she opened it and guess what!!! A very beautiful Genie jumped out!!! Yumpin' Yimminy!! Lena was so excited!! She had never seen a real, live Genie!!!!

"Oh, my, thank you!! Thank you for letting me out!!!" said the Genie. " Now you may have one wish!!! What would you like to wish for?" asked the Genie.

"Oh! My goodness!! Dat is yust vunderful!!" said Lena. "I am going tew Norvay and I am so afraid tew fly!!!" she said. "Could yew build me a bridge tew Norvay?"

"Oh, Lena!!! I am so sorry but I just don't know how to do that!!!" said the Genie. "But you may have one more wish!"

"Vell, okay," said Lena. "I vill be looking fer a nice and very, very smart husband when I get tew Norvay!! Could yew make a very, very smart Norwegian man fer me?" asked Lena.

"Oh, my, no, Lena!!!!" exclaimed the Genie. "When should I start the bridge????"

*** *** ***

"I yust don't know vhat tew dew vit my daughter, Ingrid!!" said Pete. "Vhen she drives da car she goes yust like lightning!!!"

"Vell, dew yew mean dat she drives fast?" asked Sven.

"Vell, no, Sven!!" said Pete. "She hits trees!!!"

*** *** ***

"Eat yer spinach, Little Pete!" said MaMa Hilda. "It vill put color in yer sheeks!!!"

"Vell, MaMa!! Vhy in da vorld vould I vant green sheeks?????"

*** *** ***

Lena was giving advice to the new bride!! "Gertrude," she said. "Give Gunner a fish and he vill eat fer a day! But if yew get somevun like Ole tew teach him tew fish, yew vill get rid of him every veekend!!!"

*** *** ***

For some unknown reason Ole got the idea that his wonderful wife, Lena, was hard of hearing, so one day he asked from across the room: "LENA, CAN YEW HEAR ME?" Lena didn't answer so he moved closer and yelled, "LENA, CAN YEW HEAR ME?" Still no answer so Ole moved even closer! "LENA, CAN YEW HEAR ME?" Still dear Lena didn't answer!!! Poor Ole was getting really worried so he moved right behind Lena and yelled, LENA, CAN YEW HEAR ME!!!!!!"

This time Lena responded in a very loud voice, "YES, OLE, I HEAR YEW FER DA FOURT TIME!!!!!!!!!!"

*** *** ***

"Little Sven, vhy are yew crying?" asked Grandpa.

"Vell, yust because Daddy von't play cowboys and Indians vit me tewday!!" sobbed Little Sven!

"Vell, don't cry!!" said Grandpa. "I vill play cowboys and Indians vit yew!!!"

"But dat's no good, Grandpa!!!" sobbed Little Sven. "Yew've already been scalped!!!!"

*** *** ***

A policeman pulled Hjelmer over, jumped out of the police car and came running over!!!!

"Good Gracious, Man!!! Didn't yew realize that your wife fell out of the car two miles back?" he yelled.

"Vell, tank goodness fer dat!!!" exclaimed Hjelmer. "I taught dat I vas going deaf!!!!"

*** *** ***

OLE SAYS, "DERE ARE TREE VAYS TEW GET SOMETING DONE:
                  1. DEW IT YERSELF
                  2. HIRE SOMEVUN TEW DEW IT
                  3. FURBID YER KIDS TEW DEW IT!!!!!!

*** *** ***

Ingvar went to an auction and after some very heavy bidding, he got the bid on the parrot!!! He was so excited!!! He had spent his very last dollar on the parrot!!!! Poor Ingvar didn't have a cent left in his wallet!!!

"Vell, can he talk?" he asked the auctioneer as he picked up the parrott.

"Talk!!!!" exclaimed the auctioneer!!!! "JUST WHO DO YOU THINK WAS BIDDING AGAINST YEW !!!!!!!"

Lars walked into a store and told the clerk that he would like to buy 5 pounds of Lutefisk!!!

"Oh!" said the clerk! "Are you Norwegian?"

Lars became very indignant and replied, "Hey, if I had asked fer pasta, vould yew have asked if I vere Italian? If I had asked fer sauerkraut, vould yew have asked if I vere Yerman !!! If I had asked fer tacos vould yew have asked if I vere Mexican!!!!"

"Well, no sir!!!" replied the clerk.

"Vell, den, vhy in da vorld did yew ask me if I vas Norvegian yust because I asked fer lutefisk?!!!!" yelled Lars.

"Just because this is a hardware store, sir!!!" was the clerk's reply!!!

*** *** ***

Little Ole had grown up a bit and he was now a teenager who had just learned to drive!!! He was so proud of his new found driving ability!!! One day he invited Mama Lena to go for a ride with him!!

"How vunderful fer Little Ole tew vant tew take his mudder fer a ride!!!" she thought. But just about then Little Ole turned off onto a narrow mountain road!!!! Of course Lena thought he was going a little too fast!!!!

"Little Ole!" she said softly. "I feel yust a little bit nervous vhen yew go around vun of dose sharp bends so fast!!!"

"Oh, don't yew vorry, MaMa," replied Little Ole. "Yust shut yer eyes like I dew!!!!"

*** *** ***

It was income tax time so Pete walked into the tax office one day! He had a huge bandage on his nose!!!!!

"Vell, Pete!!! It looks like you had a bad accident!!" said the tax collector.

"Vell,no! I didn't!!" replied the grumpy Pete. "I've yust been paying tru it fer so long dat it gave vay under da strain!!!"

*** *** ***

LENA SAYS: "Dere is vun good ting about getting old!!!
Yew can sing all yew vant tew in da batroom
vhile yew are brushing yer teeth!"

*** *** ***

Hilda competed with a French woman and an English woman in the Breast Stroke Division of an English Channel Swim Race!!! The French woman came in first and the English woman came in second!!! Poor Hilda finally reached shore completely exhausted!!!

After Hilda was wrapped in a blanket and was drinking hot coffee, she remarked, "I yust don't like tew complain, but dose udder two vomen ver using dere arms tew!!!!!"

*** *** ***

When Selmer accidentally dropped a quarter down the outhouse hole, he immediately threw his watch and billfold down!!!!

"Vell, vhy in da vorld vould yew dew dat?" asked his friend Peter.

"Vell, are yew stupid or something!!!" yelled Selmer. "Dew yew tink dat I am going down dere fer yust twenty five cents!!!!!"

*** *** ***

Young Ingrid brought her fiancé home to meet her folks! After dinner her father took Ingvar into his study for a chat.

"So vat are yer plans, son?" he asked.

"Vell, sir! I am a theology scholar," replied the young man.

"Vell, dat is vunderful, son!!" exclaimed Ingrid's father. "But vat vill yew dew tew provide a nice home fer my dear daughter?"

"Vell, sir! I vill study and God vill provide!!" explained the young lad.

"Yes, God will provide!!" said Ingrid's father.

The two men left the study and of course MaMa Selma could hardly wait to question her husband!!!

"Vell, how did tings go, dear?" she asked.

"Vell, it's dis vay, Selma!!! He has no employment plans, but on da udder hand he tinks I'm God!!!"

*** *** ***

"Vell, Daddy! I am yust so tired!! Vill yew dew my homevork fer me?" asked young Hans.

"Vell, yew know dat I yust can't dew dat, son!!! It vould yust be wrong!!!!!" exclaimed his father.

"Vell, dat vould be okay yust as long as yew give it yer best effort, daddy!!!!" declared the yawning child!!!

*** *** ***

Ole says, "Vell, I have finally reached financial independence! Novun vill loan me any money!!!!"

*** *** ***

Little Ole was watching a news special and became very excited one evening!!!

"Yumpin' yimminy, Dad!!!" he exclaimed!!! Did yew know dat Micheal Yordon has a whole country named after him?"

*** *** ***

"NO!!! NO!!! Little Lena!!! I yust don't tink dat e-mail vould be better den saying yer prayers!!!" scolded MaMa Lena!

"But vhy not?" asked the child. "Doesn't God have a computer?"

*** *** ***

It was a wicked winter in Northern Minnesota and would you believe that Ole and Lena and Sven got lost in the woods!!! Well, they did!!! The snow was very deep and still coming down!! Several days earlier they had run out of food!! Things were looking mighty bleak for Ole, Lena and Sven!!

All of a sudden Sven had an idea!! "Ve vill dig vay down in da snow and dere vill sure be some nuts down dere dat ve can eat!!!" So they all started digging and digging with their hands!!!! And they were getting so cold!! They were about to give up when >>> would you believe it >>> A GENIE popped her head out of a snow bank!!!

"Uff-da!!" she said. "Are yew cold and hungry?? Vell, tewday is yer lucky day!!! I am da great SNOW GENIE OF NORDERN MINNESOTA and I can get you out of dis awful bad situation!!! Soon yew vill be varm and have vunderful lutefisk and lefse tew fill yer tummies!!! I know dat yew are so cold and hungry! I vill grant yew each vun vish!! Vat vill yer vish be, Ole?"

"Vell," said Ole. "I vish dat I vas back on da farm!!" POOF! POOF! >> and Ole was gone!!!

"Now, Lena!! It is yer turn tew make a vish! Vat vill yer vish be, Lena?" asked the great SNOW GENIE OF NORDERN MINNESOTA !!!"

"Vell," said Lena. "I am yust so lonesome fer mine Ole!! I vish dat I vas back on da farm vit Ole!!!" POOF! POOF!! >> and Lena was gone!!

Poor Sven was sitting there looking so sad!! Finally, the great SNOW GENIE OF NORDERN MINNESOTA said, "Sven, you look so sad!! Now it is yer turn tew make a vish!!! Vat dew yew vish fer, Sven?"

"Vell," said Sven. "I've been tinking about dat and I am yust so lonely!!! I vish dat Ole and Lena vere back here vit me!!!"

*** *** ***

Ninety-five year old Hans was in great health for his age. He was still alert of mind and got around by himself very well!!!! However, he felt it was necessary to resist the determined advances of a lovely widow some thirty years younger!!

"Mudder and Fadder are bot against it!!!" he explained to the lady.

"Vell, Uff-da!!!" shrieked the lady. "Uff-da!! Uff-da!! And more Uff-da's!!! Yew are not going tew tell me dat dey are still living, are yew?!!!"

"Vell, no!! Quite da contrary!!!" Hans replied. "I am just refering to Mudder Nature and Fadder Time!!!!"

*** *** ***

Hjelmer showed up for work one day with a big black eye!!!!

"Vat in da vorld happened tew yew, Hjelmer?" asked Sven.

"I've got seenus trouble!!" replied Hjelmer.

"Vell, yew must mean sinus trouble!!" corrected Sven.

"Vell," said Hjelmer. "All I know is dat I vas out vit anuder voman and my wife seenus!!!!"

11

The good pastor went to the hospital to visit elderly Inga after the doctors had removed her last three teeth!!! He munched on a bowl of peanuts she had sitting by her bed as he visited with her, and to his embarrassment, he consumed the whole bowl!!

"Vell, I am so sorry dat I munched all yer peanuts, Inga!!! I promise tew bring yew more peanuts tomorrow!!!" he said.

"Oh dat's okay, Pastor Yon!! But if yew dew bring me more peanuts tomorrow, make sure yew bring da shocolate covered kind, because all I can dew is suck the shocolate off and spit da nuts in dat bowl!!!!"

*** *** ***

Petra complained bitterly and constantly!!! "Yew yust don't dew a ting tew help me around da house and I even have tew dew all da yard vork 'cuz yer yust out dere at da golf course all da time!!! I am yust sick of doing all da vork around dis place!!!"

Finally Petra's good for nothing husband had enough of his wife's nagging!

"Petra!!" he snapped! "I dew a lot more den golf!!! Now vill yew please pass da putter?!!!!!"

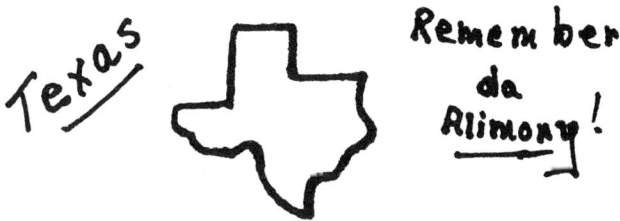

Texas 🗺️ Remember da Alimony!

Lena, the young teacher, had just presented a long lesson on the history of Texas to her attentive students.

"What was the famous battle cry that later helped gain the independence of Texas?" she asked.

Little Lars quickly raised his hand!!!!

"Vell, teacher!" he declared. "It vas 'REMEMBER DA ALIMONY!!!!!'"

*** *** ***

"Father, is it a sin tew play golf on Sunday after shurch?!" asked Peter on his way out of the church on Sunday morning.

"My Son," the priest replied! "I've seen you play golf! It's a sin any day!!!!"

*** *** ***

LENA SAYS: UFF-DA IS VATCHING A NON-SCANDINAVIAN AT A CHURCH SUPPER USING LUTEFISK FER A NAPKIN!!

*** *** ***

HOW ARE YEW RELATED TO WHOM????????

LENA SAYS: Ve all know dat a shild of yer mudder's or fadder's brudder is yer first cousin! And a shild of yer first cousin is yer first cousin once removed!! Not yer second cousin!

A shild of yer first cousin once removed is yer first cousin twice removed!!!

Yer second cousin is a shild of yer grandparent's brudder's or sister's grandshild!!! Yer second cousin's shild is yer second cousin once removed; and that shild's shild is yer second cousin twice removed!!!

VELL, YUST TAKE A BREAK AND AN ASPIRIN AND DEN VE VILL CONTINUE!!

Yer turd cousin is yer great-grandfadder's or yer great grandmudder's brudder's or sister's great grandshild!! Yer turd cousin's shild is yer turd cousin once removed!!!

"VELL," says Lena!! "DAT'S YUST ABOUT ENOUGH TEW CONFUSE BOT GOD AND EINSTEIN!!!!"

*** *** ***

Grumpy Olga was bitten by a dog with rabies!!! Uff-da! Later she told her friend, Lena about it!!!
"Vell, Olga!" said the excited Lena. "I yust tink dat yew had better start writing yer vill!!"
So Olga began to write! She wrote and wrote and wrote some more!!!!
"Dat's a pretty long vill, isn't it, Olga?" asked Lena!!
"Vell!! Who's writing a vill!!!" snapped Olga! "Dis is a list of people dat I am going tew bite before I die!!!!"

*** *** ***

"Do you believe in life after death, Ole?" asked his boss one morning when he arrived at work.
"Vell, yes, sir!! I sure dew!!" was his quick reply.
"That's good," said the boss. "After you left early yesterday to go to your grandmother's funeral, she stopped in to see you!!!!"

*** *** ***

Dear Friend Hilda,

I have become a little older since I saw yew last and a few shanges have come into my life since then!! Frankly, I have become quite a frivolous old gal!! I am seeing five yentlemen every day!!!!

As soon as I vake up, Vill Power helps me get out of bed!!! Den I go tew see Yon!! Den Sharlie Horse comes along and vhen he is here he takes a lot of my attention!! Vhen he leaves Artur Ritis shows up and stays the rest of the day!! He doesn't like tew stay in one place very long, so he takes me from yoint tew yoint!! After such a busy day, I'm really tired and glad tew go tew bed vit Ben Gay!!! Vhat a life!!!

Love, Lena

P.S. Da preacher came tew call da udder day. He said dat at my age I should be tinking about da hereafter! I told him, "Oh! I do all da time. No matter vhere I am… in da parlor, in da kitchen, in da batroom or on da porch, I alvays ask myself 'Vat am I here after???"

*** *** ***

Pete confessed to his pastor, "I have stolen a shicken, sir!! Vould yew like tew have it?"

"Vell, certainly not," said the pastor!! "I will not accept stolen goods. You must return it to the one you stole it from!!"

"Vell," said Pete. "I offered it tew him and he refused!!"

"In that case you might as well keep it yerself!!!" replied the pastor.

Pete said, "Thank you, sir!!" and hurried away.

The pastor then returned home to find one of his chickens missing!!!!

*** *** ***

"Dad, I have decided tew leave home and yoin a traveling theater group!!!," said young Sven.

"Vat!!! A son of mine on stage!!!" yelled PaPa Ole.

"Vell!! I vill shange my name den!!!" said Sven.

"Shange yer name!!!" yelled PaPa Ole. "Vat if yew are a success? How vill da neighbors know dat it's my son?!!!"

*** *** ***

Olga was trying to return the short handled back scratcher that she received as a Christmas gift. The clerk was shocked!

"Olga!" she said. "It's not a back scratcher! It's salad tongs!"

*** *** ***

LARS SAYS: VHEN I TRACED MY FAMILY TREE,
I FOUND OUT DAT I AM DA SAP!!!

Dear Petra,

Dis is a line tew say dat I am living and not among da dead, though I'm getting fergetful and mixed up in da head!!!! Fer sometimes I can't remember when I stand at da foot of da stairs... if I must go up fer someting or if I just came down from dere!!! I stand before the refrigerator so often! My poor mind is filled vit doubt! Have I yust put something avay or have I come tew take it out? And there are times when it is dark out, with my nightcap on my head, that I don't know if I'm retiring or yust getting out of bed!! So if it's my turn tew write, dere's no need fer getting sore!! I may tink dat I have written and don't vant tew be a bore!!! So remember dat I love yew and I vish yew vere here!! But now it's nearly mail time, so must say—

Goodbye My Dear!
Yer Friend, Lena

P.S. Here I stand before da mailbox with a face so very red!!Instead of mailing yew dis letter, I have opened it instead!!!

*** *** ***

Ole took his dog to the vet. After examining the dog, the Vet said, "I'm so sorry Ole! Your dog is dead!!!"

"Vell," Ole said. "I vant a second opinion!"

So the vet called in a cat. The cat walked around and the dog didn't move!!!!

"Well, what do you think, Ole?" asked the vet.

"Vell," said Ole. "I guess yew vere right, Doc!! My dog is dead!!!"

So the vet presented Ole with a bill for $350!!!

"Vell, Uff-da!!!" said Ole. "Vhy in da vorld is dat bill so big, Doc?"

"My bill is only $50 Ole!!" said the vet. "The $300 is for the 'Cat Scan!!'"

*** *** ***

Lena rushed into the police station!! "I have yust been robbed!!!" she yelled.

"Calm down lady!" said the police chief. "Describe the robber for me! Did he have a mustache?"

"Vell, I'm not too sure!" said Lena. "But if he had vun he must have shaved it off!!!

*** *** ***

HANS SAYS, "MIDDLE AGE IS WHEN YEW CHOOSE YER CEREAL FER DA FIBER INSTEAD OF DA TOY!!!!!!!!!!

*** *** ***

SMILE

A SMILE COSTS NOTHING BUT GIVES MUCH!! IT ENRICHES THOSE WHO RECEIVE IT, WITHOUT MAKING POORER THOSE WHO GIVE!

IT TAKES BUT A MOMENT, BUT SOMETIMES IT LASTS FOREVER.

NO ONE IS SO RICH OR SO MIGHTY THAT HE CAN GET ALONG WITHOUT IT... AND NO ONE IS SO POOR THAT HE CANNOT BE MADE RICH BY IT.

A SMILE CREATES HAPPINESS IN THE HOME, FOSTERS GOOD WILL IN BUSINESS, AND IS THE COUNTERSIGN OF FRIENDSHIP.

IT BRINGS REST TO THE WEARY, CHEER TO THE DISCOURAGED, SUNSHINE TO THE SAD, AND IS NATUR'S BEST ANTIDOTE FOR TROUBLE.

YET IT CANNOT BE BOUGHT, BEGGED, BORROWED OR STOLEN, FOR IT IS SOMETHING THAT IS OF NO VALUE TO ANYONE UNTIL IT IS GIVEN AWAY.

SOME PEOPLE ARE TOO TIRED TO GIVE YOU A SMILE.

GIVE THEM ONE OF YOURS, AS NO ONE NEEDS A SMILE MORE THAN HE WHO HAS NO MORE TO GIVE!!!!

– Author unknown –

*** *** ***

OLE SAYS, "HE WHO LAUGHS LAST DIDN'T GET DA YOKE!"

*** *** ***

After beginning a very prestigious job, Ole had to report for some special training. His wife, Lena and their three year old daughter, Tina, were driving him to the training site.

"Mommy! Vere are ve going?" asked Little Tina.

"Ve are taking Daddy tew training!" answered Lena.

With a strange look on her face, Little Tina said, "Potty?"

*** *** ***

UFF-DA IS HAVING LASAGNA AT A LUTEFISK SUPPER!!!!!

*** *** ***

Kjell bought his wife a beautiful diamond ring for Christmas! His friend, Olaf said, "I thought she wanted one of dos pretty four vheel drive vehicles!"

"Vell, she did!!" replied Kjell. "Bur vhere in da vorld vas I going tew find a fake yeep?!!!"

*** *** ***

Olga went in for an interview for aa position on the Lutheran Church staff!!

The Pastor read over Olga's application and then he said, "I see yer birthday is April l5, Olga! What year?"

Olga quickly replied, "Vell, every year, Pastor!!!"

*** *** ***

Pete was a very wealthy businessman who always came home from work, sat in his easy chair and read the paper as his wife, Hilda prepared dinner and set a lovely table in the dining room with the family china and silver!! Of course she always had a beautiful centerpiece of beautiful fresh flowers!!! What a woman!!!

One day he sat in his easy chair and read the paper and when he came to the local gossip column, he became very upset!!!

"I yust can't believe dis, Hilda!!!! It says right here in dis gossip column dat yew packed up and left me!!! Have yew ever in dis vorld heard anyting so absurd, Hilda?!!!! >>> HILDA >>> HILDA!!!!!! VERE ARE YEW, HILDA?!!!!!!!!"

*** *** ***

LENA SAYS: DA MOST COMPLETELY LOST OF ALL DAYS,
IS DAT ON WHICH ONE HAS NOT LAUGHED!!

*** *** ***

Pastor Lars was so distressed over the abundance of saloons in his community and the widespread drinking among his flock, that one Sunday morning, he preached a very long sermon against drinking liquor and frequenting the saloons!

"I vish dat dere vere no saloons in dis vorld and dat dere ves no such ting as liquor!!" he declared. "I wrote tew da President of da United States of America and asked him tew give me a permit tew enter all da saloons and carry out stores and gadder up all da bottles filled vit dat nasty, awful, terrible stuff!!"

"Vhen I get dat permit," he continued, "I am going tew empty all da vhisky kegs, bust all da beer bottles and pour all dat liquor in da river, and by Thanksgiving Day yew vill see dat river flowing high vit all dat sinful stuff!!"

"Vell," he continued. "Now I have said my piece!! Now let da choir sing!"

The choir director raised her baton, the organist sounded the chord and the choir members rose to their feet and sang. "Shall We Gather At The River!!"

(This is said to be a true story!!!!)

*** *** ***

Lena had a sink full of dishes and there was a power outage!! Let's call Grandma! She knows how to vash dishes!!" said little Ole!

*** *** ***

*** UFF-DA, NEI-DA and FY-DA ***

Almost everyone is acquainted with the Scandinavian expression "UFF-DA", but not so many people know about "NEI-DA"and "FY-DA!!! Adding these expressions to your vocabulary can enrich it immensely, and with proper usage, you will never be at a loss for words!! However, these words must be used properly!!! They are not to be used as a substitute for cuss words; they are simply used when special emphasis is required!!!!

UFF-DA expresses compassion, empathy, or annoyance! You can safely say UFF-DA when your co-worker slams a finger in the door, when you walk into a door, or when your mouser drags a dead rat into the kitchen!!!

NEI-DA is used on occasions when you are surprised or shocked in a negative way, or when something happens that you can hardly believe!! It is perfectly proper to say "NEI-DA" if your property taxes go up a 100% or if someone tells you that Santa Clause is going to wear a Hawaiian shirt this Christmas!! NEI-DA is also used when you tease someone, and this person asks you if you really meant what you said!!!

FY-DA (fee-da) expresses disgust, revulsion, horror or more!!! It is reserved for very special occasions, such as when your dog gets sprayed by a skunk, or the six-year-old slips and falls in the barn gutter!!! In some cases, FY-DA is equivalent to "shame on you!!" It can be used jokingly, like when the man you are in love with, steals a kiss and you need to say something to hide your sheer uncontrollable delight!! It can also be used in scornful reproach!! For instance, when your dog triumphantly brings home all the newspapers in the neighborhood!!!!

A true Scandinavian-American knows something awful has happened when someone exclaims "FY DA MEG"!! The only modern day expression that even comes close to the meaning of "FY DA MEG" might be "OH!! YUK!!"

UFF-DA! It must have been awful for non-Scandinavians to grow up without these helpful expressions at hand!!! Now that you have been filled in on their uses, you will know how to use them often and fittingly!!!!! After all, this great ethnic tradition must go on!!!

*** *** ***

LENA SAYS: Da secret of being boring
is tew tell everyvun everyting!

*** *** ***

"Vell, yew know it is really hard tew believe," said Little Ole to Little Sven! "But my mom said dat all mudders used tew be little girls!!! Can yew believe dat!!!"

*** *** ***

Olga was a night nurse at the hospital and one evening a bomb threat was recieived!! The nurses were told to check the patients rooms for anything that was suspicious! Tina carried a flashligh and entered the room of 85 year old Bridget, who was sleeping... So Tina carefully tiptoed and began to poke around near a box of candy!

Suddenly Bridget woke up!! "Vell, Uff-da!!" she exclaimed!! "If yew vanted a piece of candy, all yew had tew dew was ask!!!"

*** *** ***

Ole went into the office to see his boss! "Sir," he said. "Ve are having tew dew some heavy house cleaning tomorrow and my vife needs me tew help vit da attic and da garage >> Yew know, moving and hauling stuff!!!"

"No! Ole! Yew can't have the day off!! We are short handed right now!!!!" says the boss.

"Gee, tanks, Sir!!" says Ole. "I yust knew dat I could count on yew!!!"

*** *** ***

Lars sat down with his cereal bowl and said to his good vife, Hilda, "Vell, dear, I decided tew eat healthy from now on!! Tewday, I am having OATMEAL!!!"

Oh, that's good dear!!" said Hilda.

After a few bites Lars said, "I sure hope dat I can dewelop a taste fer dis stuff!!! It goes down really rough!!"

"Vell, how long did yew cook it?" asked Hilda.

"Vhat!!! Yer supposed tew cook it!!!" yelled Lars!

*** *** ***

Yew have yust received da Sven and Ole computer virus! Because we don't know how tew program computers, dis virus vorks on da honor system!!!

Please delete all yer files on yer hard drive and forvard dis message tew everyvun on yer mailing list!!! Tanks fer yer cooperation!!!

*** *** ***

NEWS FLASH!!!! PETER PETERSON, LOCAL NORVEGIAN COMPUTER EXPERT, REPORTED DAT HE HAS SUCCESSFULLY COUNTERED DA SVEN AND OLE VIRUS VIT DA LENA AND BIRGETTA ANTI-VIRUS SOFTWARE!!!! IT APPEARS DAT DIS CONVERTS DA SVEN AND OLE VIRUS INTO LUTEFISK, WHICH IS NOT DESTRUCTIVE TO ANYTING EXCEPT THE HUMAN DIGESTIVE SYSTEM!!!

*** *** ***

Young Sophie was on a long trip and traveling in the winter! Guess what happened!!! She had car trouble. She was stalled by a big building, so she rang the doorbell!!!

To her surprise, a Catholic monk answered the door! They were just sitting down to supper. They kindly asked her to join them and she had a delicious supper of fish and chips!!!

When the meal was finished, they gave her a tour of the house and when they came to the kitchen, Tina met the cooks! They were Brother Ole and Brother Jens!!

"Vell, vat good cooks yew are!!" said Sophie.

"Tank yew!" said Brother Ole. "I am da fish friar!!!"

"Yes," said Brother Jens. "And I am da chip monk!!!"

*** *** ***

Pete and Hilda were lost in New York City and it was getting dark and of course, Pete was getting very grumpy!!!

"Vell, dear!" comforted Hilda. "Ve may be lost but ve are making wary good time!!!"

*** *** ***

Tina went into the post office and asked for five dollars worth of stamps.

"What denomination?" asked the clerk.

"Vell!! Uff-da!!!" said Tina. "I yust don't tink yew should be asking questions like dat!!! But if yew must know, I'm Luteran!!"

*** *** ***

Poor Pete was really down in the dumps and he was telling his friend, Lars his troubles!!

"My vife yust doesn't understand me? Does yers?" asked Pete.

"Vell, I yust don't know!!" said Lars. "I've never heard her mention yer name!!!!"

*** *** ***

Petra and Peter were celebrating their first wedding anniversary!! So Peter bought Petra a new cell phone!! WOW!! WAS SHE EXCITED!!!!!!

The next day she was out shopping when the phone rang!!!!

"Hi, Sveetheart!!" said her husband. "How dew yew like yer new phone?"

"Vell, I yust love it!! It's so cute and small and yer voice sounds so clear!" declared Petra. "But dere is vun ting dat I yust don't understand!!!"

"Vell, vat is dat?" asked Peter.

"Vell, how did yew know dat I vas at Val-Mart!!!?"

*** *** ***

Ole went into the grocery store. He really likes the owner's quick wit and intelligence.

"Tell me, Mr. Olson! What makes yew so smart?" he asked.

"Vell, Ole!" he said. "Yew know dat I vouldn't share my secrets wit yust anyvun! But since yer such a good friend and faithful customer, I'll let yew in on a little secret!!! IT'S FISH HEADS!! If yew eat lots of dem yew vill become vary brilliant!!!"

"Uff-da!!" said Ole. "Vell I suppose dat I could try dem!!!!! Dew yew sell dem here?"

"Oh, ya sure, ve do!!" said Mr. Olson. "Yust $4.00 each!!"

Well, Ole bought three and away he went!!! He vas so happy!

A week later, Ole returned to the store. He was not happy!!! "Vell, dey didn't dew me any good, Mr. Olson!!" he complained.

"Vell, yew yust didn't eat enough!!" said Mr. Olson.

So Ole bought 20 more fish heads!!! Two week later he returned and he was really fightin' mad!!!

"Hey, Olson!!" he yelled. "Yer selling me fish heads fer 4 bucks each!!!! I can buy a whole fish fer $2.00!!! Yer rippin' me off!!!"

"Vell, see!!" said Mr. Olson. "Yer getting smarter already!!"

HILDA SAYS DAT DESE ARE REALLY DA TRUE SIGNS OF AGE

Everyting hurts and vhat doesn't hurt, doesn't vork!!!

Yew feel like da night after vhen you haven't been anywhere!!!

Yew get vinded playing shess!!!

Yer shildren begin tew look middle aged!!!

Yew look forvard tew a dull evening!!!

Yew turn out da light fer economic radder den romantic reasons!!!

Yew sit in a rocking shair and can't get it going!!!

Yer knees buckle and yer belt vont!!!

Yer 17 around da neck, 42 around da vaist, 96 around da golf course!!!

Yew yust can't stand people who are intolerant!!!

Yew burn da midnight oil until 9 pm!!!

Yer back goes out more often den yew dew!!!

Yer pacemaker raises the garage door vhen yew see a pretty girl!!

The little gray haired lady you help across the street is yer vife!!!

Yew get yer exercise acting as pallbearer fer friends who exercise!!!

Yew have too much room in da house and not enough in
da medicine cabinet!!!

Yew sink yer teeth into steak and dey stay dere!!!

*** *** ***

OLE SAYS: VAT'S ALL DA FUSS ABOUT INWENTING A CAR
DAT DOES AVAY VIT GAS! VE OWN VUN ALREADY!

*** *** ***

"Dese used tew be grapes," said Hilda to Little Tina as she gave her a handful of raisens!!
"Vat happened?" asked Tina. "Did yew put dem in da dishvasher?"

*** *** ***

Tillie belonged to a diet club and was telling her friends at club that she had gained weight and she was not happy about it!!!!

"Vell," she said. "I made my family's favorite cake fer my birthday and dey ate half of it!!! Da next day I kept staring at da udder half, until I finally cut a tin slice fer myself! And den I cut anuder tin slice and den anuder until it vas all gone!!! I vas so sad and ashamed of myself!!!"

"What did your husband say when he found out?" asked her best friend.

"Vell, he didn't find out!" said the smiling Tillie. "I yust made anuder cake and ate half of it!!!!"

*** *** ***

Peter was newly married and one day he asked, "Kitra, vould yew have married me if my fadder hadn't left me all dis money?"

"Vell Honey!" replied Kitra sweetly. "I vould have married yew no matter who left yew da fortune!!!"

*** *** ***

Ole, Sven and Lars were all patients at the Mental Hospital! The administrator decided the men should be returned to society, so he called them into his office!

"Well, fellows! You need to pass this test before we can release you! Ole, you are first! What is the total of 6 plus 2?"

Ole replies, "27,000"!!!

"We need to think about that!!" said the administrator. "Now, Sven, you are next! What is 6 plus 2?"

Sven replies, "Vednesday!!!"

"We need to think about that!!" said the administrator. "Okay, Lars, it is your turn!!" declared the administrator. "What is 6 plus 2, Lars?"

"Vell," said Lars! "Dat is easy! I took da 27000 and diwided it by Vednesday and da answer is 8!!!!!"

*** *** ***

Hilda's dog was scratching something awful, so she took him to the vet!!

"I will have to give this dog a shot of medicine!!" said the vet. The very smart dog understood what the vet said, and he ran likity-split right out of the vet's office—and across the street into the used car lot! Of course Hilda ran right after him!!!

The car salesman saw Hilda in the used car lot, so he asked, "May I help you, Maam?"

"Vell, no, sir! I am yust looking fer my itchy poochie!" said Hilda.

"Vell, I'm so sorry, Ma'am!!" replied the salesman. "We just don't have any foreign cars by that name for sale in this car lot!!"

*** *** ***

Little Lars came home form kindergarten one day!! He was really excited!! "Mom! I am da smartest kid in my class!" he said.

"Yumpin' Yimminy!!!" said Mom! "Did yer teacher tell yew dat, son?"

"Vell, no!! She didn't!" replied Little Lars. "Dat's cuz she doesn't know it yet!!!!"

*** *** ***

The pretty young nurse was in Ole's hospital room one day and Ole thought "Wow! Vhat a purty nurse!!!"

"Dew yew tink dat I vould be vell enough tew take yew tew dinner next Sunday?" he asked.

"Vell!" said the young Scandinavian nurse. "I tink dat yew should ask my fiancé!! He vill be operating on yew tomorrow!!"

*** *** ***

Hans was really getting disgusted with all the traffic at his lake cottage, where parking spots are few and far between!! Soon he decided to put up a sign that said, "No Parking Here!" Wow!!!

He really meant it!! A few days later he made another sign that said, "No Turning In Driveway!!!" Finally, he added a third sign. It said, "No Cutting Trough Da Yard!!!"

Well, his neighbor, Lars, had really had enough of Hans's grumpiness, so he put up his own sign!!! It said, "And Don't Come Over Here Eider!!!

OLE SAYS: IN DA GOOD OLD DAYS DERE VAS SOMETHING
TEW MAKE YEW SLEEP AT NIGHT!!!
DEY CALLED IT VORK!!

*** *** ***

Sven was rip snortin' mad!! "Vitch vun of yew pushed da outhouse over!!" he yelled!

"It vas me, Pa," said Clem.

"Vell, son!! Come into da voodshed!!! I am going tew tan yer hide good!!!" yelled Sven!

"But, Pa!" exclaimed Sven. "George Vashington's Pa didn't whip him when he told the trut about da sherry tree!!!

"Vell, dat's true, son!!" replied father Sven. "But vhen he cut down dat sherry tree, his fadder vasn't sitting in da branches!!!

*** *** ***

LENA SAYS: SQUARE MEALS OFTEN MAKE ROUND PEOPLE!!

*** *** ***

Kjell's false teeth were torturing him all day!! "Dis is awful! "I yust can't stand my false teeth tewday! Dey hurt yst terrible bad!"

"Well, try these!" said a man he had yust met!

"Uff,da!!! Dese hurt yust awful bad tew!!" said Kjell as he gave them back to his new found friend!

"Here's another pair! They might work for you!" declared the new friend.

"Oh, my! Dese are yust vunderful!! Dey don't hurt at all!" said Kjell!! "Yew must be a dentist!! How much dew I owe yew?" he asked.

"Glad to help you out!" said the friend. "There is no charge! I am the undertaker!!!"

*** *** ***

Gertrude says, "I am yust so tired of arguing vit my teen-age son about borrowing da family car!! I've decided da next time dat I vant it, I vill yust take it!!"

*** *** ***

The convention was long and drawn out!! The speakers had been really boring and dull and poor Ole had yust had enough! And what do you suppose happened!! You guessed it!! He was asked to give the Blessing!!! He was really too tired to think and so he bowed his head and said,

"NOW, I SIT ME DOWN TEW SLEEP
DA SPEAKER'S DULL, DA SUBJECT DEEP!
IF HE SHOULD STOP BEFORE I VAKE,
GIVE ME A YAB, FER GOODNESS SAKE!!!"

*** *** ***

"Well," said Jens's doctor. "The best thing for you to do is to give up smoking, drinking, running around and golf, and to keep very strict hours!!"

"Vell, Doc!" said Jens "I don't really deserve da best!!! Vat's second best?"

*** *** ***

Hilda vent to the dentist with a very bad tooth ache!!! "How long will it take tew pull my tooth?" she asked.

"It will just take about two minutes!!" replied the dentist.

"Vell, how much vill it cost?" she asked.

"I charge $50 to pull a tooth." was his reply!!

"Vell, dat's terrible!!" shrieked Hilda. "You sharge $50 fer only 5 minutes vork!!"

"That's right!!" said the dentist. I could pull it very slowly though!!!"

*** *** ***

A beautiful young Selma rushed into the psychiatrist's office! "I'm yust so in love vit a vunderful man and he's in love vit me!!" she declared! "Our parents approve of da marriage and we feel certain dat ve vill be happy!!!

"Well, that sounds wonderful!!" said the psychiatrist. "What's your problem?"

"Vell, doctor," she moaned. "I yust don't know vhat tew tell my husband!!!!"

*** *** ***

LENA SAYS: Humor is da shortest distance between two people!!!

*** *** ***

Ole moved to an Irish community and he was the only Lutheran in town! Everyone else was Catholic! They all got along very well except on Friday nights. Ole would be out at his grill fixing a steak when everyone else was eating fish!!!

Being good Catholics, the town people convinced Ole that he should convert to Catholicism. At church on the special day, Ole knelt before the priest.

"You were born a Lutheran , you were raised a Lutheran, but now, Ole," said the priest as he sprinkled the insence, "Now you are a Catholic!"

Ole's friends thought all was fine, until the next Friday night! They could smell steak cooking on Ole's grill!! They decided it was their duty to go talk to him about it!!

However, as they got closer to Ole standing by his grill, they overheard him say, "Yew were born a cow, yew were raised a cow, but now," he said as he sprinkled salt on it, "Now yew are a valleye!"

*** *** ***

Ole is da kind of guy who always hits the nailsquarely on da thumb!!

*** *** ***

PETE SAYS: MY VIFE HILDA HAS A SLIGHT SPEECH DEFECT! YA, EVERY VUNCE IN A VHILE SHE STOPS TEW BREATHE!!!

*** *** ***

Little Sven said, "I am yust so tough dat I vear out a pair of shoes in vun veek!!!"

"Vell, I'm so tough dat I can vear out a pair of jeans in yust vun day!!!" said Little Lars.

"Oh! Dat's notting!! Yew guys aren't so tough!!" said Little Ole!! " I vear out bot Grandpa and Grandma in yust vun hour!!!"

*** *** ***

"Vhat dew yew mean dat I don't know how tew keep house?" asked Tina. "I've been divorced tree times and every time I kept da house!!!"

*** *** ***

"DEAR GOD! I AM YUST TOO TIRED TEW TALK TEWNIGHT!!!" declared Little Lena. "DEW YEW SUPPOSE DAT YEW COULD YUST RECYCLE VUN OF MY PRAYERS!!!!"

*** *** ***

Poor Ole was locked out of his car on a bitter cold winter's night in North Dakota!! He was so disgusted with himself for leaving his keys inside his car!!!

Lars just happened to come by and he said, "Vell, Uff-da!! Vhere is yer udder set of keys, Ole?"

"Vell, Lars! Lena has dem!!" replied the disgusted Ole!

"Vell, vhere is Lena?" asked Lars.

"Oh, she's in da car!" declared Ole!!!

*** *** ***

What would the average woman rather have – beauty or brains ????
Lena's Answer: Beauty!! Yust because the average man can see
better den he can tink!!"

*** *** ***

"Look! It's a milk grinder!!" said Lil
when she saw the cream seperater!

*** *** ***

Olga says: Live long enough tew be a problem tew yer kids!
Get Even!

*** *** ***

Hilda Says: Da best kind of meals in my brand new cook book
are dose vunderful kinds dat I don't have tew cook!!

*** *** ***

"I can fit over vun hundred spread sheets into my hard drive!" boasted
Ole, the accountant.

"Vell, big deal! I can fit more den a hundred contracts on my hard
drive on my computer!" boasted Lars, the lawyer.

"Vell, dat's nothing!" said Pete, the scientist! "I can fit over ten
tousand formulas on my hard drive!"

"Vell, yew folks don't know nutin' about hard drives," piped up a
stranger named Sven, who had joined them. "Uff-da! I can fit more den
vun hundred tousand oranges on my hard drive!"

"Oranges?" the accountant asked. "Vat kind of hard drive dew yew
have?"

"Florida tew New York, tvice a veek!!" was his quick reply!

*** *** ***

Lars, Pete and Ole were sitting in the maternity ward at the local
hospital! They were all pacing the floor as a nurse entered and she said,
"Lars Larson, "Congratulations! Your wife just had twins!"

"Vell, dat is something!!" said Lars. "Dew yew know dat I vork fer da
Twins Baseball Team, and now I have twins!!!"

Just about then, another nurse came in and she said, "Pete Peterson!!
Congratulations! Your wife just had triplets!"

"Vell, vat dew yew tink about dat?" said Pete. "I vork fer da Tripple A,
and now I have triplets!"

He had no longer gotten the words out of his mouth, when the third
expectant father fainted!!

"Well, I wonder what ever caused him to faint?" the nurse inquired of the other men.

"Vell, I tink he yust got too excited," said Ole. "Vhen ve vere wisiting we talked about our yobs, and he said he vorks fer 7-UP!!!"

*** *** ***

Lena went to a movie and it was filled with excitement and suspence!! Suddenly Lena began looking for something under her seat!!!

"Well, what have you lost?" asked the man seated next to her.

"A caramel," replied Lena.

"Well!!!" exclaimed the man. "And you are causing all this commotion for just one caramel!!!!!"

"Vell, ya, sure yew betcha I am!!" snapped Lena! "My teeth are in dat caramel!!!!"

*** *** ***

NORVEGIAN MEDICAL TERMS

ARTERY – DA STUDY OF PAINTINGS!!!
BARIUM – WHAT YEW DEW VHEN CPR FAILS!!!
CEASARIAN SECTION – A DISTRICT IN ROME!!!
COLIC – A SHEEP DOG
COMA – A PUNCTUATION MARK
CONGENITAL – FRIENDLY
DILATE – TO LIVE LONG
FESTER – QUICKER
G. I. SERIES – BASEBALL GAMES BETWEEN SOLDIERS
GRIPPE – A SUITCASE
HANGNAIL – A COAT HOOK
MEDICAL STAFF – A DOCTOR'S CANE
MORBID – A HIGHER OFFER
NITRATE – LOWER THAN THE DAY RATE
NODE – WAS AWARE OF
OUTPATIENT – A PERSON WHO HAS FAINTED
POST – OPPERATIVE – A MAIL CARRIER
PROTIEN – IN FAVOR OF YOUNG PEOPLE
SECRETION – HIDING ANYTHING
SEROLOGY – STUDY OF ENGLISH KNIGHTHOOD
TABLET – A SMALL TABLE
TUMOR – AN EXTRA PAIR
URINE – OPPOSITE OF YER OUT
VARICOSE VEINS – VEINS VHICH ARE WARY CLOSE TOGEDDER

*** *** ***

Olga was babysitting her granddaughter!! "So much fun to have her here with me!" said Olga to herself.

Just then she spotted little Tina with her hand in Olga's big cookie jar!!

"Vhat vould yer mudder say if she knew dat yer ver getting into da cookie jar vitout Grandma's permission? Does she let yew eat cookies at home vhenever yew vant?" asked Grandma Olga.

"Oh, she say's it's OK, Grandma!" said little Tina.

"Vell, we will check vit her vhen she comes back!" said Grandma. "And yew may be in trouble if yew are fibbing!!"

"Vell, maybe I had better put dese back!" said Little Tina. Sometimes, Grandma, I yust don't hear wary vell!!!!!

*** *** ***

Poor Sophie sat on a street corner in New York City selling pretzels from a card board box. She had her little booth for twenty years and every day a man came by and gave her 25 cents, but he never took the pretzels!!

One day he put his quarter down and rushed off !! Hilda yelled at him, "Come back here, son!"

"Well, I know you want to know why I leave a quarter every day and never take any pretzels," said the man.

"Vell, no!! Dat's not vhy I called yew back!!! I vanted tew tell yew dat da price has gone up tew 50 cents!!!" replied Sophie!!!

*** *** ***

Ole and Lena were beginning to have a few problems with their memory, so they got in the habit of writing everything down!

One day Lena said to Ole, "Vould yew mind getting some ice cream fer me?"

"No Problem, Lena!" said Ole as he headed for the kitchen.

"Vell, Ole! Yew had better write it down or yew vill ferget!!"

"Vell, no, I von't !! It's ice cream! How in da vorld could I ferget dat, Lena!" he snapped. And off he went to the kitchen.

A few minutes later Ole walked back into the living room carrying a tray with eggs, coffee, cereal and orange juice!!

"Vell!!" sighed Lena. "Ole, I told yew tew write it down!!! Now look!!! Yew fergot da toast!!"

*** *** ***

Little Tina was complaining!!! "First, I got tonsillitis and den I got pneumonia and next dey gave me hypodermic and isolation!"

"Vow!" exclaimed Aunt Hilda. "My goodness! Did you ever have a hard time!!"

"I sure did, Aunt Hilda!" exclaimed Tina. "I taught dat I vould never pull tru dat spelling bee test!!!"

*** *** ***

Hilda kept running out to her mailbox about every half hour!! Finally, her neighbor, Lena, could not control her curiosity, so she walked over to visit with Hilda.

"Hi, Hilda" she said. "Yew must be expecting something wary interesting from da postman tewday!! I have seen yew run out tew yer mailbox about six times!!! Are yew expecting someting extra special?"

"Vell, no! I'm not expecting someting special !!! But my computer keeps telling me dat I've got mail!!!" replied Hilda.

*** *** ***

HANS SAYS: YEW KNOW DAT YEW ARE GETTING OLD
VHEN YEW GET DA SAME SENSATION FROM A
ROCKING SHAIR DAT YEW USED TEW GET
FROM A ROLLER COASTER!!

*** *** ***

I'M YUST FINE

DERE IS NOTING VATEVER DA MATTER VIT ME!!
I AM YUST AS HEALTHY AS I CAN BE!!
I HAVE ARTRITIS IN BOT MY KNEES...
AND VHEN I TALK, I TALK VIT A VHEEZE!!!
MY PULSE IS VEAK, MY BLOOD IS TIN...
BUT I'M AWFULLY GOOD FER DA SHAPE DAT I'M IN!!!!

I TINK DAT MY LIFE IS OUT OF WHACK!!!
AND A TERRIBLE PAIN IS IN MY BACK...
MY HEARING IS POOR AND MY SIGHT IS DIM!!
MOST EVERYTING SEEMS OUT OF TRIM!!!
DA DOCTOR SAYS DAT MY DAYS ARE FEW...
AND EVERY VEEK HE FINDS SOMETHING NEW!!
DA VAY I STAGGER IS A CRIME...
I'M LIKELY TEW DROP MOST ANY TIME!!!
BUT I'M AWFULLY GOOD FER DA SHAPE DAT I'M IN!!!!

SLEEPLESSNESS I HAVE NIGHT AFTER NIGHT...
AND IN DA MORNING I AM YUST A SIGHT!!!
MY MEMORY IS FAILING, MY HEAD'S IN A SPIN...
AND I'M PRACTICALLY LIVING ON ASPIRIN!!!
BUT I'M AWFULLY GOOD FER DA SHAPE DAT I'M IN!!

DA MORAL OF DIS TALE VE UNFOLD...
DAT FER YEW AND ME WHO IS GROWING OLD...
'TIZ BETTER TEW SAY, "I'M FINE VIT A GRIN...
'CUZ 'TWILL SURELY HELP DA SHAPE DAT VE'ER IN!!

From the files of Lola Melton

*** *** ***

There was a knock at the door and Lena quickly answered it. She found her old high school friend standing there with a big, big dog!!!

"Vell, Tillie!!"she said, "I am so happy tew see yew!!! My goodness!!! It has been years since I last saw yew vhen ve vere graduating from High School!!!"

They had a wonderful visit!! Talking over old times was so much fun!!! But the big dog was anything but polite and was tearing around da house and he even knocked over a antique vase and broke it!!!! Lena was a little bit mad about that!!!!!

Finally, Tillie said, "Vell, dis has been vunderful, but I really must be going!!!"

"Yes, so good tew see yew!!!" said Lena. "Don't ferget yer dog now, Tillie!"

"Dog?" said Tillie. "I yust don't even have a dog!! I taught it vas yers!!!!!"

*** *** ***

Poor Ole had been very sick and finally, one sad day, he died! St. Peter met him at the pearly gates of Heaven!

"Hello there, Ole," said St. Peter. "Nice to see you! We do have a few questions that you will have to answer before we can let you enter Heaven though! Are you ready for this little test, Ole?" he asked.

"Oh, ya, sure!" said Ole. I vas a wary good student vhen I vas young!!! I'm yust sure dat I can answer dos questions! Vat's da first vun?"

"Okay, Ole! Here is the first question!" said St. Peter. "How many 'T's in a week?"

"Oh, dat's easy!" said Ole. "Dat's tewday and tewmorrow!!"

"Very good" said St. Peter. "How many seconds in a year? Can you answer that for me, Ole?"

"Oh, ya, sure! Dat's Easy!" replied Ole. "Dere are twelve! Da second of Yanuary, Da second of February, Da second of March, Da second April, Da second of May, Da second of Yune, Da second of July, Da second of August, Da second of September, Da second of Otober, Da second of November, Da second of December! Dat is twelve seconds in vun year

"Well, okay! Ole!! I have one more question for you! Are yew ready for the last question, Ole?"

"Oh, ya, sure, I'm ready," said Ole.

"Well, here it is," said St. Peter. "What was Jesus first name?"

"Oh! Dat's an easy vun!" said Ole. "Jesus first name vas Andy!"

"What?????" said St. Peter!!!!

"Andy!!" repeated Ole. "Yew know!! Andy valks vit me, Andy talks vit me!!!"

Contributed by Gordon Wallin

Lars got a job as a cowhand and he was really excited about being on a dude ranch. The very first day, he was told to 'saddle up' and he could hardly wait to get on his horse!! So he got out the new saddle and got right to work!!

"Hey, cowboy!" yelled one of his pals! "Aren't yew putting yer saddle on backwards?"

"Vell," said Lars. "Dat's all yew know about it. Yew don't even know vhich vay I'm going!!!!"

*** *** ***

"Vill yew all please write down da name of yer very favorite hymn?" asked the Sunday School teacher.

Everyone started writing and handed in their paper very soon, except Little Petra.

"Vell, Petra! Vill yew please hurry and write down yer favorite hymn?" said the teacher. "Hurry, and bring me yer paper!"

Petra finally wrote with downcast eyes, and she handed her paper to the teacher! It read 'Ole Olson'!!!

*** *** ***

Young Peter was talking about something that happened a few months earlier, and his Daddy couldn't remember what it was!

Peter got so disgusted that he went to his mother and said, "Dad's got sometimers, MaMa!!! Sometimes he can remember and sometimes he can't remember!!"

*** *** ***

"Teacher!" said little Ole. "I yust don't vant tew scare yew, but my daddy says if I don't get better grades, somebody is going tew get a spanking!!!"

*** *** ***

LENA SAYS: HAPPINESS IS A GREAT BIG SMILE!!!
LAUGH AND DA VORLD LAUGHS VIT YEW,
CRY & YEW CRY ALONE!

*** *** ***

An elderly spinster, Gertie, passed away last month. Since she had never married, she requested "NO MALE PALLBEARERS!!" In her hand written instructions for her memorial service, she wrote—"Dey vouldn't take me out vhen I vas alive!! I von't have dem taking me out vhen I'm dead!!!"

*** *** ***

Ole was a brand new police recruit! During his exam, he was asked, "What would you do, Ole, if you had to arrest your own mother?"

"Vell," replied Ole. "Da first ting dat I vould dew vould be tew call fer backup!!!"

*** *** ***

Little Peter went to Sunday School every Sunday!! The Sunday School teacher told them that God created everything, including people!!

"Yes, that is right!! Did you know that Eve was created from one of Adam's ribs? Well, that is true!" she said.

Later that week, MaMa Lena found Little Peter lying down in his bed early in the day!

"Peter, are yew sick?" she asked.

"Vell, I have a pain in my ribs," he said. "I tink dat I am going tew have a vife!!!

*** *** ***

Little Peter was very dirty when he came in from playing outside!! He found his mother in the kitchen, and he immediately asked, "Who am I, MaMa?"

His mother thought he was playing a game, so she said, "I yust don't know!!! Who are yew?"

Little Pete started to sob, "Da neighbor lady vas right!!! She said dat I vas so dirty my own MaMa wouldn't recognize me!!!!"

*** *** ***

OLE SAYS: "ADAM AND EVE HAD A VUNDERFUL
                  MARRIAGE!! HE DIDN'T HAVE TEW
                  HEAR ABOUT ALL THE MEN SHE COULD
                  HAVE MARRIED, AND SHE DIDN'T HEAR
                  ABOUT DA VAY HIS MUDDER COOKED!!!!"

*** *** ***

Lena is a wonderful driver, of course!! However, on several occasions, she had been stopped by a highway patrolman, and her explanations are something to laugh about!!!

"Vell, officer!! I vas yust trying tew kill a bee, vhen I ran into dis telephone pole!!!!"

"An inwisible car yust came out of nowhere, struck my car, and den it disappeared!!!"

"Vell, it vasn't my fault!!! A stationary truck collided vit me, coming da udder vay!!!"

"I vas on da vay tew da doctor vit rear end trouble, vhen my uniwersal yoint vent out!!!"

"I had been driving my car fer 60 years, vhen I fell asleep at da vheel and landed in da hospital!!"

"Da pedestrian yust didn't have any idea vhitch vay tew go, so I yust ran over him!!!"

Here's Ole's best excuse for an accident! I yust pulled away from da side of da road, looked over at my mudder-in-law, and headed over da big dropoff!!!"

*** *** ***

It does seem that almost everyone has a computer these days!! Some of terms used appear to be a little strange, especially when used by those of us who have a bit of a Scandinavian accent!!! The following comes from the "NACA News" and the author is unknown.

"Computer Terms" {as read by Grandpa Anderson}
****

Log On: Makin' da vood stove hotter!!
Log Off: Don't add no more vood!!
Monitor: Keepin' an eye on da vood!!
Download: Getting' da vood off da truck!!
Mega Hertz: Ven yer not careful gettin' da firevood!!
Floppy Disc: Vat yew get from trying tew carry tew much vood!!
Ram: Dat ting dat splits da vood!!
Hard Drive: Gettin' home in da vinter time in da snow!!
Prompt: Vat da mail ain't in da vinter time!!
Vindows: Vat yew shut vhen it's cold outside!!
Screen: Vat tew shut vhen it's black fly season!!
Byte: Vat dem dang black flys do!!
Chip: Munchies fer da TV!!
Microchip: Vat's in da bottom of da munchies bag!!
Modem: Vat yew did tew da hay fields!!
Dot Matrix: Old Dan Matrix's Vife!!
Laptop: Vhere da kitty sleeps!!
Keyboard: Vhere yew hang da keys!!
Software: Dem dang plastic forks and knives!!
Mouse: Vat eats da grain in da barn!!
Mainframe: Holds up da barn roof!!
Port: Fancy vine!!
Random Access Memory: Ven yew can't remember vat
    yew paid fer da rifle, vhen yer vife asks!!

*** *** ***

TALE A BOUGH – AN ODE TEW DA SPELLING CHEQUER!!!!
Original by Janet E. Byford (minus da brogue}!!!!!

Praise da Lord fer da spelling chequer
    Dat comes vit out pea sea!!
Mecca miss stake and it puts yew rite
    It's so easy tew use, yew see!!
I never used tew no, vas it e before eye?
    For sometimes it's eye before e!!
But now I've discovered, da vay tew success
    Is as simple as vun, two, free!!
So vhat if yew lose a letter or two,
    Da vorld von't come tew an end!!

Can't yew see it's as plain as da nose on yer face
Spelling Shecker's my wary best friend!!
I've alvays had rubble vit letters dat double!!
"Is it vun or two 'S's I'd vhine
But now as I tolled yew, dis chequer is great
And it's hi thyme yew got vun like mine!!!

*** *** ***

Ole and Lena had just gone to bed one night, and of course the phone rang!!! Ole jumped out of bed and ran to answer the phone and Lena heard him yell, "Vell, how in da vorld vould I know dat??! Dats two tousand miles avay from here!!!!" and he hung up and went back to bed!!

"Vell, who vas dat?" asked Lena.

"Vell, darned if I know!!" replied Ole. "Some crazy fellow vants tew know if da coast is clear!!!!"

*** *** ***

A Norwegian man, a Swedish man and a Negro man were all sitting in the waiting room of a maternity ward, and they were very anxiously awaiting the birth of their babies!

The doctor finally came out, but he said, "I'm so sorry, but we got the three beautiful babies all mixed up!!"

The nurse came out then with the three babies!! It was decided that the Swedish man should choose which baby was his first, so he choose the black baby!!

"Well, why in the world would you choose this beautiful black baby?" asked the nurse!!

"Vell," replied the Swede. "I yust vanted tew be sure dat I didn't get da Norvegian!!!

*** *** ***

Little Tena called her grandmother with some very special news!! "Guess vhat Grandma," she said. "I lost my bottom toot! Now I have vindows in my SMILE!!!!"

*** *** ***

Lena is always good at giving advice!! She says, "Yew must alvays go tew udder folks funerals!!!! Uddervise dey von't come tew yers!!!"

*** *** ***

Little Oscar was sitting on the front porch as his brother and his girlfriend drove up in front of the house. His big brother jumped out of the car, ran around to the other side, and opened the door for his girlfriend!!

Little Oscar turned to his friend Pete, who was sitting beside him, and said, "My brudder alvays has tew dew dat!! She's really pretty but she's not wary strong!!"

*** *** ***

QUEEN LENA'S MOTTO: YUST KEEP SMILING!!
IT YUST MAKES EVERYVUN VONDER VHAT YER UP TEW!!!

*** *** ***

Beautiful Hilda was on vacation and she found a wonderful place to sunbathe, high on the roof of her hotel. She wore a new bathing suit the first day, but on the second day, she decided that no one could see her anyway up there, so she slipped out of her suit to get an overall tan!!!

Hilda just barely got settled, when she could hear someone running up the stairs!! She was lying on her stomach, so she just quickly covered her fanny with the towel!

"Excuse me, miss," said the flustered assistant manager of the hotel, who was completely out of breath from running! "Dis hotel doesn't mind yew sun bathing on da roof, but ve vould appreciate yew veering a bathing suit as yew did yesterday!!"

"Vell, vat difference does dat make?" asked Hilda!! "Novun can see me up here anyvay!! Besides, I am covered vit a towel!!"

"Vell, not exactly!!" said the embarrassed young man!!!! "Yew're lying on da skylight!!!"

*** *** ***

The following announcements were found in the church bulletin:

Da cost of attending da Fasting and Prayer Conference includes meals!!!

Miss Lena Larson sang, "I Vill Not Pass Dis Vay Again," giving obvious pleasure tew da congregation!!!"

Ladies!!! Don't ferget da rummage sale!! It is a shance tew get rid of all dose tings dat are not wort keepin' around da house anymore!!!

Da peacemaking meeting scheduled fer tewday has been cancelled, due to a conflict!!!

Tillie remains in da hospital and needs blood donors for more transfusions! She is having trouble sleeping and requests tapes of Pastor Jack's sermons!!!

Pete Yohnson and Petra Peterson vere married October lst in da shurch shapel. So ends a friendship dat began in dere school days!!

Fer dose of yew who have shildren and don't know it, ve have a nursery down da stairs!!!

Da ladies of da shurch have cast off clothing of every kind! Dey may be seen in da basement on Friday afternoon !!!

Da ladies Bible study vill be held on Thursday morning at 10!!! All ladies are invited to lunch in da Fellowship Hall after da BS (Bible Study) is done!!!

Da Low Self Esteem Support Group vill meet Thursday at 7PM. Please use da back door!!!

Veight Vatchers vill meet at da First Presbyterian Shurch on Thursday at 7PM. Please use da large double doors at da side entrance!!

Da Associate Minister unveiled the church's new tithing campaign slogan last Sunday: 'I UPPED MY PLEDGE – UP YERS!!!'

*** *** ***

The minister, Pastor Ole Olson, was speaking to his flock from the pulpit on Sunday morning:

"Dis morning I am going tew talk about da relationship between faith and fact!!

"It is a fact dat yew are sitting here in shurch!! It is also a fact dat I am speaking!!!

"But it is faith dat makes me believe dat yew might be listening tew vhat I have tew say !!!"

*** *** ***

LENA SAYS: WRINKLES MERELY INDICATE
VHERE DA SMILES HAVE BEEN!!

SMILE

IT DOESN'T MATTER HOW GROUCHY YER FEELING,
YEW'LL FIND A SMILE MORE OR LESS HEALING!!
IT GROWS IN A WREATH, AROUND YER FRONT TEETH
THUS PREVENTING DA FACE FROM CONGEALING!!

*** *** ***

Ole was really upset!!! In fact he was downright mad at his son, Pete, who had been told to call home if he was going to be out past his curfew time!! Ole had dozed off in front of the TV, and when he woke up there was still no sign of Young Pete!!

"Vell," Ole said tew himself! "I vill yust see vhat dat kid is up tew!!!" and as he got more angry by the minute, he punched in Pete's cell phone number!!

Pete answered, and Ole snapped. "Vere are yew and vy haven't yew bodered tew phone?!!!!"

"Dad!! I'm upstairs in bed!!!" replied a sleepy Pete!! I've been home fer an hour!!!"

*** *** ***

Ole and Lena were running errands three days before their wedding day and they were involved in a head on collision and killed instantly!!!

Well, they stood before St. Peter at the Pearly gates and asked him if they could still be married as they had planned.

"Vell," said St. Peter (he must be Norvegian) "Not tewday!! But sheck back vit me later!!"

A few days went by and the couple again asked St. Peter if he would marry them. Again he refused and he did so many times after that!!

Finally, ten years later St. Peter agreed to let them marry, and two years later Ole and Lena decided that things just were not working out for them!! So they approached St. Peter and asked him to grant them a divorce!!

St. Peter looked at them with disgust!! Finally, he said, "Vell, it took me 10 years tew find a pastor in Heaven tew marry yew!!! How in da vorld dew yew expect me tew find a lawyer??!!"

*** *** ***

QUEEN LENA SAYS: AlVAYS BE NICE TEW YER SHILDREN
BECAUSE DEY VILL SURELY BE DA VUNS TEW CHOOSE
YER NURSING HOME!!!!!!!!!!!!!!!!!!!

*** *** ***

Ole was a dentist in North Dakota!! He put up this sign!!!
"PATIENT PARKING ONLY!! ALL OTHERS WILL BE
PAINFULLY EXTRACTED!!!

*** *** ***

Ole and Lena were celebrating their golden wedding anniversary!! They went out for dinner at a fancy restaurant, and then they came home and sat by the fireplace hand in hand and talked about their wonderful fifty years of marriage!!

"Yew know vhat, Lena!!!" said Ole. "Yew are still my sveetheart, after all dese years!! In fact, I've never had anudder sveetheart, because I've never found anyvun as sveet and beautiful as yer are!!"

"Ole," replied Lena. "Yer as big a liar as ever and I believe yew yust da same!!!"

*** *** ***

The photo finishing shop received a reprint order from Lars Larsen! The photo he had sent was an old black and white photo of a man milking a cow! The man was sitting behind the cow and all that was visible of him were his legs and feet!!!

However, Lars had sent a note with it giving printing orders!! It said, "Dear Photo Man, Dis is da only photo dat I have of my Grandfodder! Please move da cow so dat I can see vat he looked like!!!"

Young Gunder was in kindergarten and he was enjoying a vacation day with his grandmother.

"Tew day is Lincoln's birthday!" said Grandma.

"Vell, ya! I know dat!" said Gunder.

"Abraham Lincoln was the president of our country!" added Grandma.

"Vell, ya, I know dat!!" said little Gunder. "Ve learned dat in school yesterday!"

"But dat vas a long time ago!!" continued Grandma. "He isn't president now!"

"I know dat, Grandma!" Gunder answered impatiently. "He's a statue!!!"

*** *** ***

41

LENA SAYS: I YUST HAVE A VUNDERFUL MEMORY!
DERE ARE ONLY TREE TINGS DA I CAN'T REMEMBER!!!
FACES, NAMES AND I CAN'T REMEMBER DA TURD TING!!!

*** *** ***

"Grandpa! I vas yust vondering who told yew how tew drive before yew married Grandma??" said Little Sven!

*** *** ***

"Ve vent tew da ballet da udder night!" said Hjelmer, "and dere is vun ting dat I yust can't figure out!!"

"Vat's dat?" asked Ole.

"Vell, all dose girls vere dancing on dere tip toes!!" said Hjelmer. "I don't know vhy in da vorld dey don't yust get taller girls!!!"

*** *** ***

Tillie noticed her good husband, Thor, standing on the bathroom scale, sucking in his stomach!! Thinking that he was trying to weigh less with that maneuver, she commented "Vell, honey! I yust don't tink dat is going tew help much!!"

"Vell, sure it does!!" he replied. "It's da only vay dat I can see da numbers!!!!

*** *** ***

"Dad, I tink dat I deserve a new car fer graduation dis spring!!" remarked young Lars.

"Vell," said father Pete, after much thought. "I vill get yew dat new car if yew dew tree tings!!! Get better grades, read da Bible more and get a haircut!!!"

Just before graduation, the son asked his father, "Vell, Dad, how am I doing? Have yew decided dat I vill get da new car?"

"Vell, son! Yew've brought up yer grade average from a D to an A and dat's yust great!!" said good old Dad. "And I've also noticed dat yew have been reading da Bible vunce in a vhile and dat is vonderful!! But yew still haven't cut yer hair!!!!!"

"But, Dad," moaned the young man! "Vhile I vas reading da Bible, I noticed dat Moses is alvays pictured vit long hair. Even Jesus had long hair!!!!"

"Dat is true!" replied his father. "But yew must remember dat vas den and dis is now!!! And also yew must remember dat Jesus valked everyvhere he vent!!! And yew vill too, unless yew get dat hair cut!!!!"

*** *** ***

When Lena Dunn heard Sven was leaving Norway to go to the United States, she asked him to check on her son, who hadn't written since moving to New York a few months earlier!!! Lena didn't know her son's address, but Sven promised to do his very best to find him!!

Arriving in New York City, Sven was quite overwhelmed, but he was attracted to a big, shiny building with a sign saying 'Dunn and Bradstreet!'

It sounded right to Sven, so he went right inside to the information desk.

"Dew yew have a Yohn here?" he asked.

"Yes, sir!" replied the secretary. "Down the hall and the first door on your left!!!"

As Sven entered the room, he saw a man who was drying his freshly washed hands.

"Are yew Dunn," asked Sven.

"Yes, sir!!" said the man.

"Vell, son!" said Sven, "Yer supposed tew call yer mudder!!"

*** *** ***

LENA SAYS: "UDDER PEOPLES TROUBLES ARE NEVER SO
BAD AS OURS, BUT DERE SHILDREN ARE ALVAYS
A LOT VORSE!!!"

*** *** ***

Lars showed up in church one Sunday morning with his ears bright red and blistered!!!

"Vat in da vorld happened tew yew, Lars?" asked the pastor.

"Vell, dis is vat happened, I vas lying on da couch yesterday afternoon vatching da Wiking football game on TV, and my vife, Olga vas ironing in da front of da TV so dat she could vatch tew!!"

"Vell," continued Lars. "I vas yust totally enyoying da game vhen da phone rang!!! And as I vas keeping my eyes glued tew da TV, I grabbed da hot iron and put it tew my ear!!!"

"Vell, Uffda!! Dat is terrible," said the pastor!! "But, vhat in Heaven's name happened tew yer udder ear?"

"Vell," said Lars! "I had no more den hung up da phone, and dat same guy called again!!!"

*** *** ***

Pete was applying for insurance, and the agent asked, "Did you ever have an accident, Pete?"

"Vell, no!" replied Pete

"Then you've never been hurt! Is that right' Pete?" asked the insurance agent.

"Vell, a dog bit me vunce," replied Pete. "But dat vasn't any accident!! Da dog vas mean and he definitely did it on purpose!!!"

*** *** ***

Grandson, Ole, was eyeing with wide eyes, the wedding picture of his grandparents:

Grandma!!" he exclaimed. "Dis is a funny picture! Grandpa isn't veering his glasses and he has his hair on!!!"

*** *** ***

"Vasn't dat nice dat all yew shildren got a treat after Bible school was over yesterday, Little Hilda?"

"Oh, ya, sure, Grandma!!! Dat vas really nice and ve didn't even have tew go trickin' fer it!!!" replied Little Hilda!

*** *** ***

Katrina got her little daughter up very early on the first day of kindergarten!!! She wanted to make sure they had plenty of time for breakfast and to get dressed in her new schoool clothes! In fact it was still dark outside when she woke the child!!!

Little Katy looked very sad and unhappy!!

"Vat's da matter?" asked MaMa Katrina? "Dis is yer big day!"

"Vell, MaMa!!" said Katy "I didn't know it vas Nite School!"

*** *** ***

Ole and Lena had just retired for the night! Ole was so tired and was almost asleep when his good wife poked him with her elbow!

"Ole! Vake up! Yew used tew hold my hand vhen ve vere courting!!" said Lena.

Wearily, he reached across the bed and held her hand for a second!! And then he tried to go back to sleep!

Once again Lena poked him with her elbow! "Ole! Vake up! Den yew used tew kiss me!!" said Lena.

Ole was getting a little bit irritated, but he reached across and gave Lena a little peck on the cheek! And he tried to go back to sleep!

About a minute later Lena poked him again, with her elbow! "Ole! Vake up!" she said. "Den yew used tew nibble on my neck!!"

As you might know, Poor Ole had really had enough!! He threw off the bed clothes and jumped out of bed!!!

"Vat are yew doing, Ole?" asked Lena sweetly?

"Vell!!" snapped Ole. "I am going tew get my teeth!!!"

HILDA SAYS: HANS AND I ARE GOING TEW HAVE A SECRET
MARRIAGE!! IT'SUCH A BIG SECRET DAT I HAVEN'T EVEN
TOLD HIM YET!!!

*** *** ***

* RETIREMENT *

In da year two tousand two
My vorking days shall be all tru!!
I'll be da happiest gal alive,
Fer I shall den be sixty-five!!

Each month I vatch dose old folks grin,
Each month dere pension shecks roll in!!
Each month dey get dat pot of gold,
All simply yust fer being old!!

Whoever taught dey vould see da day,
Vhen getting old meant getting pay!!!
And if yer paying tew much rent,
Yew yust apply fer supplement!!

And if dat isn't quite enough,
Yew get all kinds of udder stuff!!
Like discounts off on bus and planes,
And den yew also get da GAINS!!

And ten percent off all yer clothes,
And Senior Rates on first class shows!!
And Travel Tours are all da rage,
If only yew are senior age!!

And housing shouldn't bother yew,
Yer O.H.C. vill help yew tru!!
And even send some younger chap,
Tew come around and fix yer tap!!

If I had known, vhen I vas tventy,
Da real true meaning of "Land of Plenty"
I vould have moved bot Heaven and earth,
Tew falsify my date of birth!!

And politicians, please take note,
You'll vish yew lost by yust vun vote!!
If I vake up in two tousand tree,
And dere's no pension left fer me!!

And vorse, if on my birt'date morn,
Old Gabriel should blow his horn!!
He'd bette plan tew keep on blowing,
'Cuz vitout my pension, I'm not going!!

*** *** ***

Grey haired Grandma was combing Little Petra's hair one day! "Yew have such beautiful black hair," said Grandma.

Little Petra looked at Grandma with wide eyes!"Vell, Grandma," she said, "Yer's is trying tew be!"

*** *** ***

It was her first night away from home, and three year old Tina was a little hesitant when it was time to go to bed!!

"Vhy are yew frowning, Tina?" asked Grandma.

"Vell, Grandma!!" she exclaimed. "I yust fergot tew bring my mom and dad!!

*** *** ***

"Mom, am I Swedish" asked Little Helga

"No, dear! You are not Swedish," said her mother. "You are German!"

Little Helga started to cry!!!

"What is the matter, Helga?" asked her mother. "Vhy are you crying?"

"Because, I don't want to be Germish!!!" was Little Helga's quick reply!!

*** *** ***

The Sunday School teacher asked her class, "Why did Mary and Joseph take Jesus to Jerusalem with them?"

"Vell, teacher, dat's easy!" said little Ole. "Dey couldn't find a baby sitter!!!"

*** *** ***

Gunner was so happy!! The preacher had just sold his horse to him and he was so excited!! The good preacher took the time to explain to Gunner that he had trained the horse well!

"Ya, Gunner!" he said. "To get the horse to go, all you have to do is say, "Praise the Lord!" And when you want him to stop just say, "Amen."

"Vell, ya, Pastor Yon! Dat's vat I vill dew!" said Gunner.

Later that day Gunner jumped on the horse and said, "giddy-up!" The horse didn't move!!! Then Gunner remembered, and he said "Praise Da Lord!!" and the horse took off at a gallop!!

"Whoa! Whoa!" yelled Gunner. But the horse wouldn't stop!! The horse was about to go over the cliff, and Gunner figured that he was going to die and go to Heaven, so he said, "Amen!"

At that the horse skidded to a stop just two feet from the edge of the ridge!! Gunner looked down at the jagged rocks far below. Happy that his life had been spared, he yelled, "Praise Da Lord!!"

*** *** ***

My Dear Good Friend,

Hello! How are yew? Ve are in pretty good condition considering da shape dat ve are in!!! Ve feel better den ve ver but not as good as ve felt before ve feel as bad as ve feel now!!! Ve have so many pains now so if anoder pain started tewday, it vould be two veeks before ve could start vorrying about it!!!

I vent tew da doctor last veek and he examined me. He felt of my pulse and den my pocketbook!!! He told me dat I had newmonia! I told him dat vas nice 'cuz I hadn't had anyting new fer a long time! He showed me a bottle of pills and he held vun up and told me tew take dis pill tree times a day!! I told him dat vood be impossible and he asked vhy it vould be impossible. So I told him dat I could get it down, but I did not know how I could get it back up so dat I could take it again!! Dis made him really mad and he called me a Scandinavian Yackass because I am Svedish!!!

Dew yew remember da old buggy? I put it out by da road and put a for sale sign on it for sixty dollars! A man stopped and said he liked it but vould pay only turty dollars fer it! Ve argued back and fort and I insisted I had tew have sixty dollars fer it and he got mad and told me tew "go yump in da lake!!!" Dis vas not very nice of him and it made me very angry! vhen I got back from da lake and found dat he vas gone.

Da udder nite Gust Yonson came tew wisit me! He vas so sad!! He said dat he and his vife Yennie ver fighting again and dis fight vas over beans!! He told me dat his vife said dat she vould not cook fer him any more because he did not like anyting dat she fixed. He said dat she said, "On Monday yew liked beans – on Tuesday yew liked beans and on Vednesday yew liked beans!! Now all of a sudden yew don't like beans!!! Vat's da matter vit yew? Get Out!!!"

Dew yew remember yer old friend Ella Vickstrom? She took a trip tew Sveden tew wisit her relatives and vhen she got back I asked her about her trip and she said she had a terrible experience!!! I asked vot happened and she said shortly after dey left New York and vere flying over da Atlantic, da captain came over da speaker system and said, "I am sorry tew tell yew dat ve have lost vun motor and ve vill be vun hour late in reaching Sveden!" Dis vas not tew bad, but he came on a short time later and he said, "I am sorry tew tell yew dat ve have lost anuder motor and ve vill be tree hours late in reaching Sveden!" She said now she began tew vorry and tew pray!!

Vell, I told her dat I could understand her concern vhen dey tot dey could crash into da Atlantic. She said dis vas not her vorry!! She vas vorried because da captain said dey vould be vun hour late vhen da first motor vent out and den he said dey vould be tree hours late vhen da second motor vent out! She said dat she vas vorried dat if anuder motor vent out dey could be stuck up dere all night!!

Now I must tell yew about my experience. Last veek I heard a terrible sound coming from da shurch!! I ran like crazy because I tot dat somebody vas getting killed or something!! Vhen I got dare I trew open da shuch door and I saw Helga Stromberg sitting at da piano and she vas doing her usual hollering vitch she calls singing! Now I understand da reason fer da terrible sounds!!! I slammed da door shut and started running avay from it!! But Helga had seen me and she ran after me and said, "Olaf! Yew heard my singing!!! Vat did yew tink of my execution?" I told her dat I am highly in favor of it!!"

Our new member, Amos Mortenson got himself in trouble vit Pastor Olson!!! Da Pastor vas showing Amos trew da shurch and dey came tew a plaque and da pastor told him dat on dis plaque are da names of all da men of da shurch dat had died in da service. Amos said, "Vitch vun? Da morning or da evening?"

Ve have decided tew build a new shurch. Our plans fer building comes from da minds of our smart business men. Ve are going tew build da new shurch right vhere da old vun sits!! Ve are going tew use da material from da old shurch tew build da new shurch!! Ve are going tew meet in da old shurch until da new shurch is built!!

I got tew close dis letter because I am suffering from a pain in my stomach and I hope yew are da same.

Yer old friend,Olaf

P. S. If yew don't get dis letter write tew me and I vill send anuder!

Written by John C. Bogren   Dec. 1998

OLE SAYS: My vife, Lena is da younges 40 year old voman dat yew vill ever meet. According tew her she is only 29!!!!!

*** *** ***

Middle Age: When the words Happy and Birthday go separate ways!!

*** *** ***

Lars and Hilda were watching the soap opera! It was very sad and the tears were streaming down Hilda's cheeks!

"Vell, Hilda !! How in da vorld can yew sit dere and bawl over the silly, make believe troubles of people dat yew've never even met?" asked Lars.

"Vell, Lars!!! Yust da same vay dat yew can yump up and scream vhen some guy dat yew've never even met scores a touchdown!!!" replied Hilda between sniffles!!!

*** *** ***

The teacher asked Little Tina, "Can yew read and write?"

"Vell, I can write," replied Tina. "But I can't read!!"

"Vell, let me see you write your name." Said the teacher.

Tina wrote on the piece of paper and gave it to the teacher.

"Vat is dis?" asked the teacher as she tried to read the scribbles.

"Vell, I don't know!!" replied Little Tina. "I told yew dat I can't read, teacher!!!!"

*** *** ***

LENA SAID: "YA, SURE!!! VE BUILT OUR DREAM HOUSE! IT COST TVICE AS MUCH AS VE DREAMED IT VOULD!!!

*** *** ***

Lars recently purchased a brand new sports car!!!! WOW!! He was so proud of his brand new car!!! He took it out for a drive one evening and soon he saw flashing red lights behind him!!

"Vell, Uff-da!!" he said to himself. "I tink dat I can outrun dat guy," and pretty soon he was going 120 miles an hour!!! All of a sudden he realized how foolish he had been !!! So he pulled over and waited while the patrolman came up to the car window.

"Sir!!" said the police officer. "Did you know that you were going way too fast!! This is the last of my night shift and I'm really tired of paperwork!! If you can give me a good reason why you were going so fast, I'll let you get by this time!!!

Lars thought for a minute!!! "Vell, sir," he said. "My vife ran off vit a patrolman yust last veek and I vas sure dat vas him trying tew catch me tew give her back!!!"

*** *** ***

Sven was being interviewed for a job as a prison guard. "Do you think you can handle this job, Sven?" asked the interviewer. "It can be very dangerous, you know!!!"

"Vell, ya, sure, sir!! I can handle it!" replied Sven. "If anyvun gives me a problem, dey are out of here!!!"

*** *** ***

Good old Pete got a job painting houses!!! He really was doing a super job!!

One day his boss came to check on him. "You are doing a fantastic job, Peter!!!!" said the boss. "But why in the world are you wearing all those jackets when it is 95 above out here?"

"Vell," replied Pete. "Just because da directions on da can says 'put on two coats'!!!"

*** *** ***

Oscarina was returning from a first aid class when she came upon a man who was sprawled face down on a very dark street!!

"Vell," thought Oscarina to herself. "I must help dis poor man who has fallen down!!! Poor fellow!!!"

She immediately rolled up her sleeves and started artificial respiration!! All of a sudden the man looked up at Oscarina and said, "Lady, I don't know vat in da vorld yer up tew!!! I am holding a lantern fer a guy vorking down in dis man-hole, and I really dew vish dat yew vould let me get on vit my vork!!!"

*** *** ***

Lena and Hilda were neighbors and they decided to go on a diet at the same time!!

"Dat is yust vunderful!" exclaimed Lena. "Ve can be dieting pals and go fer valks cuz exercize is so good fer us!!"

"Vell, ya, sure! Dat vill be so nice! Ve can help each udder out!! Vhen I get da urge tew go out fer a burger, fries and malt, I'll call yew first!!" said Hilda.

"Great!!" exclaimed Lena. "I vill go vit yew!!!"

OLE SAYS: Vhen da udder fellow takes a long time,
        he's slow, but vhen I take a long time,
        I'm thorough. Vhen da udder fellow doesn't
        do it, he's lazy; but vhen I don't do it,
        I'm too busy. Vhen da udder fellow does
        something vitout being told, he' overstepping
        his bounds; but vhen I dew it, dat's initiative!
        Vhen da udder fellow takes a positive stand
        on something, he's bull-headed; but vhen I do,
          I'm firm.
        "Vhen da udder fellow overlooks a rule of
        etiquette, he's rude; but vhen I skip a few
        rules, I'm original! Ven da udder fellow
        pleases da boss, he's polishing brass; but
        when I please da boss, dat's cooperation!
        vhen da udder fellow gets ahead, he's
        getting da breaks; but vhen I manage to
        get ahead, it's due tew good hard vork!!

"Vell, now doesn't dat give us all something tew tink about!!!

*** *** ***

It was time for a real vacation!! Ole and Lena had never had a nice vacation so they decided to take their young son Pete, and spend a weekend in New York City !!

Lena was exhausted from all their touring around the city, so she decided to go up to their room and take a little nap.

"Vell, Little Pete!" said Ole. "Let's yust take a little tour around dis beautiful hotel!!" So off they went, and soon they noticed a pair of shiny walls that could slide open and close.

"Vell, vat is dat?" asked young Pete.

"Vell, son!! I have never seen anyting like dat in my life!!" said Ole.

Just then a tacky looking woman with a crabby look on her face, walked up to the doors, pushed a button. The walls opened up and the woman stepped into a little room!! The shiny walls closed behind her. A row of lights above lit up one at a time!!! Then the walls opened and a beautiful, smiling blonde stepped out!!!

Ole and his son were dumb-founded!!!! Finally, Ole said, "Son! Go get yer mudder!!!!"

*** *** ***

Grandma was curious to know if her little grandson had learned all of his colors in pre-school. One day she decided to quiz him!!

"Vat color is dis?" asked Grandma Petra.

"Vell, dat is red!" said the child.

"Dat is right! Wary good!" said Grandma

This questioning went on with the different colors for five minutes and then Little Ole had enough!

"Vell, Grandma!!" said the child. "I tink dat yew should try tew figure some of dose colors out fer yerself!!!!"

*** *** ***

Three little boys, Sven, Lars and Ole, were in the schoolyard bragging about their fathers!!!

"Vell, my dad scribbles a few vords on a piece of paper! He calls it a poem, and dey give him $50!!!," said Little Sven!

"Vell, dat's nothing," said Little Lars. "My dad scribbles a few vords on a piece of paper, den he calls it a song and dey give him $100!!!"

"Vell," says Ole! "I got yew bot' beat!!! My dad scribbles a few vords on a piece of paper!!! Den he calls it a sermon!! And it takes 8 people vit big dishes tew collect all da money!!!!!"

Lena walked into the kitchen and found her husband, Ole, stalking around the room with a big fly swatter!!!

"Vell, vat in da vorld are yew doing, Ole?" she asked.

"Vell, voman, vat in da vorld dew yew tink dat I am doing? "I am hunting flies!!"

"Oh!!" says Lena. "Vell, are yew killing any?"

"Vell, ya, sure, I am killing dem! So far I have killed tree male two females!!!"

"Vell, Ole!!!" exclaimed Lena. "How can yew tell?"

"Vell! Lena!! Dat's easy!!" replied Old. "Two vere on da beer cans and tree vere on da phone!!!!!"

A patrolman pulls Lars and Hilda over for speeding. He walks over to the car and says, "I clocked you doing 80 miles per hour, sir!"

"Vell, Uff-da!!" says Lars. "I had it on cruise control at 60!!!"

"Don't be silly, dear," chimes in Hilda. "Dis car doesn't evenhave cruise control!!!"

As the patrolman starts to write the ticket, Lars growls at his vife, "Can't yew yust be quiet and keep yer mout shut vunce in a vhile?!!!!"

"Vell," says Hilda! "Yew should yust be happy dat da radar detector vent off vhen it did!!!"

"A radar detector!!" says the officer. "That is illegal!!!" and he begins to write up another ticket!!!!

"Darn it, voman!!!" screams Lars. "Vill yew yust keep yer big mout shut!!"

The officer bends down and looks at the woman!!! "Does he alvays talk to you like that, Maam!!!" he asks.

"Vell, Good Heavens, No!!!" Hilda exclaimed! "Only vhen he's drunk!!!!!"

Ole, Sven and Lars were traveling to Europe and they just happened to meet in a bar in Denmark!!

Ole was from the United States, Sven was from Norway and Lars was from Sweden! Well, they got pretty chummy and began to talk about their wives.

Ole from the U.S. said, "Vell, I told my vife, Lena, in no uncertain term, dat from now on she vill have tew dew her own cooking!!

Vell, da first day after I told her dat, I saw NOTHING
Da second day, I saw NOTHING!

But on da turd day, vhen I came home from vork, da table vas set vit beautiful china and a vunderful dinner was served tew me! Dere vas even dessert!!!"

It vas Sven from Norvays's turn next!! "Vell, I sat my vife down, and I told her dat from now on she vould have tew dew her own shopping and also dew da cleaning!!

Vell, da first day I saw NOTHING
Da second day I saw NOTHING!!!

But on the turd day vhen I came home from vork da whole house vas spotless and in the pantry, da shelves vere filled vit groceries!!!"

It was finally Lars from Sweden's turn and he said, "Vell, I am married to an police woman!!" He sat up straight on his bar stool, pushed his chest out and said, "Vell, I gave my vife a stern look and told her dat she vould have tew dew da cooking, shopping and da housecleaning!!"

"Vell, da first day I saw NOTHING!!
Da second day I saw NOTHING!!!!
But on da turd day I could see a little bit out of my left eye!!"

*** *** ***

Pete and Petra were having a big dinner party and they had invited many guests. When they had all sat down to the table, Petra said to their 5 year old daughter, "Vould yew like tew say da blessing fer us, dear"

"Vell, mommy!" exclaimed Little Tina, "I yust vouldn't know vhat tew say!!"

"Vell, yust say vhat yew hear Mommy say." said Pete.

Little Tina bowed her head and said, "Lord, vhy on earth did I inwite all dese people tew dinner tewday!!!"

*** *** ***

Church was over and it was time for Ole and Lena to take their children home. Pastor Olson was standing in the doorway, ready to greet each and every one of his faithful flock.

As the good pastor took his hand, little Clem said, "Vhen I grow up, I am going tew give yew some money!!"

"And vhy are yew going tew dew dat, Clem?" asked the pastor.

"Vell," replied the child. "Yust because daddy says dat yew are vun of da poorest preachers ve have ever had!!!"

MaMa Lena was preparing pancakes for her young sons, Lars and Ole. The two boys began to argue over who should have the first pancake!!!!

"If Jesus vere sitting here," said Lena. "He vould say, 'let my brudder have da first pancake!! I can vait!!"

Little Lars turned to his brother and said, "Ole, yew be Jesus!!"

*** *** ***

Poor old Rudy was really sick. In fact he was so sick that he was sure that he was dying!!! He was feverish, sick to his stomach and even his bones ached!!! He was not able to get out of bed!

One morning, however, he could smell the vonderful aroma of his favorite chocolate chip cookies!!! His vunderful vife vas baking and she vould surely bring him at least vun of dose cookies!!

Well, he waited and waited to hear her footsteps on the stairs, and he began to feel even worse!!! But he still vanted yust vun last cookie before he vent to Heaven!!

Finally, Rudy gave up on his good wife bringing him one last cookie, so he fell out of bed, crawled to the landing, rolled down the stairs, and drug himself into the kitchen where his wonderful wife, was baking cookies!

With all the strength he had left, he crawled to the table and was just barely able to lift his withered arm to the cookie sheet! As he grabbed a warm, moist, chocolate chip cookie, his very favorite kind, his wife suddenly whacked his hand with a spatula!!!!!

"Vhy did yew dew dat?" asked Rudy.

"Vell!!!" said his good wife!! "Dey are fer da funeral!!!"

*** *** ***

Ten year old Sven was having a terrible time in school!! He was failing math, English, science, geometry and even reading was hard for him!!! His parents tried everything from tutors to hypnosis!! Finally, they decided to send him to a strict religious school!!!

After the very first day at the new school, young Sven walked into the house with a stern, focused and very determined expression on his face!! He walked right past his parents, went straight to his room, and quietly closed the door!!!

For nearly two hours, he studied in his room, with math books strewn all over his desk and the floor!!!!

Finally, he emerged for just long enough to eat supper. After quickly clearing his plate, he went straight back to his room, closed the door and worked with gusto on his studies till bedtime!!!

This amazing pattern continued until it was time for his first report card!! Sven walked in with it unopened, laid it on the desk and went straight to his room!!!

Very Slowly, his mother opened it!!! To her amazement, she saw a large A under Math and all the other subjects!!

The delighted parents rushed to their son's room!!

"Vas it da teachers dat did dis vunderful ting?" asked PaPa Ole. Sven just shook his head!

"Vell, vas it da tutoring, son?" asked MaMa Lena. Sven just shook his head!

"Vell, vas it da peer-mentering and da text books?" asked Ole Sven just shook his head!

"Vell, vas it da teachers or da curriculum, son?" asked MaMa Lena. "No!!" said young Sven!!! "It vas none of dat stuff!!! It vas yust dat on da first day, vhen I valked in da front door and saw dat guy nailed tew da plus sign, I KNEW DEY VERE SERIOUS!!!"

*** *** ***

LENA SAYS: LOVE MAKES DA VORLD GO ROUND!!

Lena and Ole were having a very serious talk!!

"Honey, if I died, vould yew remarry?" asked Lena.

"Vell," said Ole. "After a considerable period of grieving, I guess I vould! Ve all need companionship!!"

"Vell, if I died and yew remarried, vould she live in dis house?" asked Lena.

"Vell, ve have spent a lot of money getting dis house yust da vay ve vant it!! I'm not going tew get rid of my house!! I guess she vould live in it!!"said Ole.

"Vell, if I died and yew remarried, vould she sleep in my bed?" asked Lena.

"Vell, da bed is brand new, and it cost us $2000!! It's going tew last a long time, so I guess she vould!!!" said Ole!!

"Vell, if I died and yew remarried, and she lived in dis house and slept in our bed, vould she use my golf clubs?"asked Lena.

"Oh, no!" replied the frustrated Ole! "She's left handed!!!!"

*** *** ***

"Vell, I finally cured Hans of biting his fingernails!!" remarked Hilda.

"Uff-da!! How in da vorld did yew dew dat?" asked her friend Olga.

"Vell, it vas really wary easy," confided Hilda. " I yust hid his false teeth!!!"

*** *** ***

Ole bought Lena a piano for her birthday and she was so excited. However a few veeks later Ole met Sven at the shopping mall.

"Vell, tell me, Ole, how did Lena like da piano dat yew bought her fer her birtday?" asked Sven.

"Oh! She really liked it!" replied Ole. "But last veek I persuaded her tew svitch tew a clarinet!!!"

"Vell, how come?" asked Sven.

"Vell," sighed Ole. "Because vit a clarinet she can't sing!!!

*** *** ***

HILDA SAYS: WRINKLES MERELY INDICATE VHERE DA SMILES HAVE BEEN!!!

*** *** ***

Lena and Hilda were always trying to lose weight!! One day Lena said, "Hilda! I made a vunderful low fat shicken dish last nite! Here's da recipe!!"

"Uff-da!" said Hilda. "It looks like it would be really bland!"

"Ya!" said Lena. "It vas until I added sour cream and sheese!!"

*** *** ***

TILLIE OLSON'S ROMANCE

Tillie Olson is a Swedish Queen Of The Kitchen who just came over from Sweden. Here Tillie reveals her past and present affair!!!

"Vell, Aye yust got over so I tank dat I drop in here fer a little vhile!! Aye mean dat I yust got over an awful excitement!!!!

Aye yust been chased by a feller!! I tank he ban trying to elope to me on account of my stylish beauty!!!

I ban come tew dis country fer tree years now tew see if I can find my sveetheart, Yon Yohnson!! But I don't can find him, so I tank dat I look around and see if I can find me a nice feller tew take da place of Yon! Yon, he ban pretty smart feller. People say he tew smart fer me tew catch!! Oh! My Goodness!!

I like tew get a nice feller like Yon vas, so vun nite last veek I vent tew da Svenska Shurch!. Dey ban having a prairie meeting every Vednesday night!

Vell, vhen da preacher says, "Everybody skol now bow dere heads" I tank dat be a good shance to look around and see if I find a nice feller in da audience! Yew bet!! I see vun!! I goin'tew make a smash on him!!!"

Ya! Yust vhen I look around, I see a nice lookin' fellow! Ya! And yust vhen I look at him, he vinks an eye like dis! (wink) Den I yust get busy and make a goo goo vink right back!!!

Purty quick he come by me and sit down by me! And he ask me if I ban alone tonight? Vhen I say, "I tank I am. Ya!" And nen he ask "Can he take me home?" He say "Dat is if yew got a home!" I say, "Vat yew tink? I live in a stabo?"

So he take me home! I tol yew he ban a nice fellow! He say I should call him Oscar, and he says dat's because it's his name!!

Vun night purty quick, Oscar took me out fer a svell time. He say he don't care fer expenses! He say he got a lot of dem, dat's vhy he don't care! Oh! He ban a good spender!! He spent money dat nite like a fish!! Oscar, he spent sixty cents dat nite!! Ten cents fer da five cent theater, tventy-five cents fer car fare and da rest fer a svell meal at da restaurant!!

By Yimminy!! Oscar don't care no more about 60 cents den he do his right eye!!! So vun night I go vit Oscar to know his mudder! Yah! His mudder ban pretty fat!! I tank every voman has da right tew be fat if she vants too, but Oscar's mudder abused her priviledge!! Vhen she came into da room, I say to Oscar, "Look Oscar! Look at da crowd dat yust came in!!" "Oscar say, "dat ain't no crowd! Dat's my mudder!!!" Dat voman! She is so cross-eyed! I yust could not tell if she vas looking fer a yob or yust vaiting fer Sunday tew come around! By Yimminy!!! But she vas a talking machine!! She gave me look over vun or two times. Den she say, "Who left da door open?" Den she started tew ask me all about Sveden!!!! If I got lots of money!!! Vat size shoe dew I vear!!! How much I pay fer my hats!!! Oh! She ban a butt in!!

Den she ask me if I got a fadder and a mudder!! I say tew her, "Lady! Dew yew tink dat I grew on a cranberry tree?!!!"

Den she say, "Yew got any brudders?" and I say, "Yes, lady!! Two living and vun married!!"

Den she got mad!!! I yust tought dat old coffee pot vould boil over!!! Her hair stood up like she had combed it vit an egg beater!!!

She say tew Oscar, "Come here, Oscar!! Vhere yew got dat fresh Svede?"

He say, "She ban fine gal, Mudder!! I got her from da shurch!"

She say, "Vell, yew can take her right back vhere yew got her or I vill trow yew bot'out!!!" Of course, I had tew go den!!!

Vell, yesterday I got inwited tew Oscar's vedding!! My clothes vill all be imported, like a sausage!!! Oscar says dat he vill get his from da ten cent store!!!

Oscar's mudder gave me a present fer my neck!! A cake of soap! Den she gave Oscar something fer his head!! It looked like a vacuum cleaner, but Oscar said it vas a shave kit!!

Tew celebrate our vedding, Oscar took me and his mudder tew da moving picture show!! Den ve vent on a boat ride. Oscar's mudder vas da heaviest ting on board so dey used her fer an anchor!! Ve sailed around fer about two hours and vhen da boat bumped up against da dock, it shook us all up purty good!! I tell yew it shook all of Oscar's mudders teeth right from her yaw!! I gave a little boy 10 cents tew pick dem up! I vas afraid dat if I picked dem up, dey might bite me!!

OH! MY! VE HAD AN AWFUL NICE TIME AT MY VEDDING!!!

Contributed by Astrid Karlson Scott

*** *** ***

Hjelmer ran into an old friend, Pete, at the coffee shop!!!

"Vell, Pete!!! I yust haven't seen yew fer such a long time! How have yew been!! Uff-da!!! Maybe I shouldn't have asked!!! Yer not lookin' so good!!!" said Hjelmer.

"Vell, I'll be okay!! I've yust had a tough year!!" replied Pete. "First my mudder died in March and left me $30,000!!! A den in April, my fadder died and he left me $50,000!!"

"Vell, Uff-da!!" exclaimed Hjelmer. "Dat is really tough tew lose bot yer mudder and yer fadder witin two months!!!"

"Vell, dat's not all!" exclaimed Pete. "Tew top it all off, my aunt died last month and left me "Vun hundred tousand dollars!!!"

"Oh! Dat is really sad!!" said sympathetic Hjelmer.

"Ya!! Tell me about it!!" said Pete. "Dis month, not a ting!"

*** *** ***

An elderly couple were on their very first trip to Hawaii! They were so excited about everything! However, there was one thing that was bothering them, so they stopped a young man on the street.

"You have such a beautiful state here and we are enjoying it so much! But there is one question we have. Could you tell us how to pronounce the name of your state? Is it Hawaii or is it Havaii?" asked the tourist.

"It is Havaii!" said the young man.

"Oh, thank you so much for telling us that!" said the visitor.

"Oh, yer velcome!!" replied the young man.

*** *** ***

Poor Ole was very sick!! In fact he was on his death bed with his dear wife Lena by his side!!

"Now Lena," said Ole. "Down in our cement block basement dere is vun block dat yew can pull out and dere is drawer full of all da good money dat I have been saving all dese years!! I vant yew tew go down dere and get all dat money and vhen I die, I vant yew tew put it all in my casket vit me!! I vant dat money vit me vhen I go!!"

"Vell, okay, Ole!! Vatever yew say I vill dew, yust like I've been doing all dese years!! Ya! I vill go find dat money now so dat I vill have it all ready vhen da time comes, Ole!!" replied Lena, and away she went to find the money!!

Lena had no problem finding the money! And as luck would be, Lena's poor dear Ole died the next morning! And, of course, Lena remembered Ole's orders to put all the money in his casket. So she rushed to the bank and deposited all the money!! Then she wrote out a check for the exact amount and rushed wildly to the funeral home and put it in Ole's casket!! What a smart Scandinavian voman!!!

NORWEGIAN BLESSING
****

MAY DA RUTS ALVAYS FIT DA VHEELS
IN YER PICKUP
MAY YER EAR MUFFS ALVAYS KEEP OUT
DA NORT VIND.
MAY DA SUN SHINE VARM ON YER LEFSE
MAY DA RAIN FALL SOFT ON YER LUTEFISK
AND UNTIL VE MEET AGAIN
MAY DA GOOD LORD PROTECT YEW FROM
ANY AND ALL UNNECESSARY
UFF-DA'S !

Author Unknown

About the author...

Charlene Power's career began as hostess of the Crosby Hour, a news, music and talk show on KTGO Radio, Tioga, North Dakota. Scandinavian jokes were a popular part of her program and eventually the collection of jokes was put into her first book, *Uff-da* (no longer printed and a collector's item).

Next came *The New Uff-da*; *Ya, Sure, Ya Betcha*; *Leapin' Lena*; *The Best of Queen Lena*; *Love, Lutefisk and Lena*; *Lena Loves Ole Jokes*; and now we have *Lena, Before and After Lutefisk*.

"Queen Lena"

Although Charlene is not Norwegian, she says there is nothing she would rather be! She was born in South Dakota among the Scandinavians and is married to a Norwegian half-breed! She and her husband, Charles, are proud of their large family – four children & spouses, eleven grandchildren and two great grands!

Charlene, also known as "Queen Lena," has been a familiar sight at Minot. North Dakota's HØSTFEST (a very large Scandinavian celebration) since its beginning twenty-five years ago. She appears as Queen Lena, just over from Norway, wearing her jello-mold crown and selling her joke books!

Charlene & Charles Power

UFF-DA

PO Box 204
Crosby ND 58730

Telephone:
(701) 965-6648

E-Mail:
uffdabooks1@
yahoo.com

QTY	TITLE	PRICE	TOTAL
	The New Uff-Da	$3.95	
	Ya, Sure, Ya Betcha	$3.95	
	Leapin' Lena	$3.95	
	Love, Lutefisk and Lena	$3.95	
	Lena Loves Ole	$3.95	
	Lena, Before and After Lutefisk	$3.95	
	The Best of Queen Lena	$9.95	
	Postage and handling		$2.00
	TOTAL (U.S. Funds)		

NAME:

ADDRESS:

CITY: STATE/PROVINCE: ZIP:

E-MAIL: